DREAMS FOR PEACE

DREAMS FOR PEACE

How the World of Dreams Can Lead Us

to World Peace

Richard Hastings

First published in 2004 by Xlibris Corporation.

Reprinted in 2008 by REGAL Publication Sdn. Bhd.

To order additional copies of this book, contact:

REGAL Publication Sdn. Bhd.
www.regal.my
orders@regal.my

Printed in Malaysia

CONTENTS

I would like to dedicate this book
in the memory of my grandmother,
Helen Kolar, who taught me about love.

ACKNOWLEDGEMENTS

I am particularly grateful for the participation of my family members especially my wife, Debby, and my two daughters, Erika and Juliet. They have been a constant source of encouragement and suggestion. All of the art work in the book has been done by Erika and Juliet.

I am also indebted to Dr. Kurt Hein who did the major revisions and editing of the texts.

I would like to acknowledge all of my students from the Maxwell International Baha'i School and my other friends in British Columbia, Canada who so graciously shared thousands of dreams with me over my 9 years there. I would like to also acknowledge my students and colleagues from the School of the Nations in Brasília, Brazil who further extended my understanding of the connection between all things.

INTRODUCTION

This is a book about peace. It isn't the typical approach to world peace. Its purpose is to show how all of our dreams, when properly understood and transformed into positive action can create a peaceful world. It doesn't put the responsibility of world peace in the hands of the world leaders, however necessary that might be, but shows how each of us are inspired in our dreaming process to make a better world.

I chose dreams just from members of my family because I wanted to show how the unity of the family translates into the same principles as unity of the world. The thesis is that united families make united communities, and united communities make united nations, and united nations make for a united world.

The world of dreams is a unified world. It has been created so that humanity can learn how to live together in harmony and peace. Everything that is taught in all of the great religious writings and by the great thinkers is also shared with us in our dreaming process. Every night that we go to sleep we are treated to a lesson on how to live a better life. It is given to us in a metaphoric way escaping the rules of space and time, and shown in both negative and positive messages. And it is perfect for us.

There are 19 dreams shared in the book. Each chapter describes the dream and my interpretation as well as some principles about dreams followed by a reflection section. The reflective part shows how the dreams of others can also help our own developmental process because in our spiritual lives we are all intimately interconnected even like being one person in many different bodies.

CHAPTER 1

"THE FIRST SHALL BE LAST, AND THE LAST SHALL BE FIRST."

Enthusiasm About Making New Friends

"So, Dad, I had this dream last night: I was somewhere visiting people and then I realized that my train was leaving right at that moment and I had to be there right then to get it. I didn't know how I could do that because I was kind of far away (anxiety). But I got there somehow and caught the train. However, it was the wrong train and so I was trying to get off, but I couldn't and it ended up taking me to the right place, a painting class. There was a big group of people and we were all waiting for the class to start. I was talking to this guy beside me and we became really good friends. The instructor started off with a dance routine with only half the people. They were dancing a certain dance in a circle. Then I was next to come and join. I still had a paintbrush in my hand with yellow paint on it, wondering what this has to do with painting, but I went along with it anyway. The instructor showed me the exact steps really quickly and I was supposed to know them perfectly and do them with everyone else . . ."

The first rule about working with dreams is that everything you know about how time and space function can be set aside. As long as you think about time only like a clock with hours and minutes and seconds and space only as measured by meters or grams or liters, you can not understand the world of dreams. The dream world has a different set of rules about time and space. It

13

includes the kind of time and space you experience in everyday life, but it also adds a lot more and uses those rules in a way to give you the kind of understanding you need to be a better person and to do something worthwhile in this world.

The first rule about space is the rule about separation. In the physical world in which we live, we make sense of things by naming things as separate and distinct objects. For instance, we know what it means when we say something is a tree or a lion. The names help us to live a less confusing life. We all have different names so that we can separate one person from another. Imagine in our everyday life if there were no such distinctions. Communication would seem impossible. As obvious as this is and as important as it is to our daily lives, in the world of dreams it is entirely possible that I can be you in a dream and you can be me. It is also possible that a tree can be a lion, and that a lion can be a tree. When you begin to open up to the possibility that things you see as distinct are really connected—as if they are the same—your dreams will begin to reveal their truth to you.

It is possible that the separations we feel in the world can be changed into feelings of closeness and harmony when we understand that the dream world is trying to bring us all closer together. We can even be like one soul in many different bodies. I use dreams of my family in this book, because all programs of peace in the world begin with strengthening the ties in families. United families make united communities, united communities make a unified nation, and unified nations make a united world. The book will show how my family's dreams are connected to the understandings necessary to have peace in the world.

The book starts with a set of two dreams from the youngest member of my family. Although she may be the carrier of a dream, the meaning of the dream has significance for us all. The Bible says that the first shall be last and the last shall be first. I am the last-born in my family, as was my mother, and her mother. The tradition of being last is very strong within us. In the material world it is usually the first son that has the tradition of the inheritance of leadership and material wealth. In the world of dreams, it is also possible that the last shall be the first and that her inheritance may be very great.

My daughter starts to explain her dream by saying, ". . . So Dad, I had this dream last night." Why is this important? In our family, in relationship to me, she is last and I am first, but in the dreams I share in this book, she is first. Whatever message she is carrying in the dream will be the first thing we will attend to as we work to achieve a more peaceful world. If we are attached to old ways of looking at the world, we will be looking for the oldest to lead the way, but she is letting us know that the last shall be the first, even as prophesized by Jesus. This also means that the young will teach the old. This is going to mean that that we need to start with youthful energy, such as the energy of enthusiasm, not "old" energy, such as wisdom. Wisdom comes later, not at the beginning.

She then says, "I was somewhere visiting people, and then I realized that my train was leaving right at that moment and I had to be there right then to catch it. But I didn't know how I could do that, because I was kind of far away (anxiety). But I got there somehow and caught the train."

In this section she is showing us that it is possible to break the barriers of time. Most people think that it takes a long time to change, a long time to get anywhere in your life, because they think about life in terms of how long it used to take. If you ask the older generations about how long it will take to change, they usually say that it takes a long time. For young people, change happens quickly. If we take the example of youth, we can make things happen more quickly.

She has some anxiety because she thought she was far away. This anxiety continues in the next part when she says, "However, it was the wrong train, and so I was trying to get off, but I couldn't, and it ended up taking me to the right place, a painting class." Even though she is young and has youthful energy and made it on time, she thinks she is on the wrong train because the former laws of how to get somewhere and how to change (e.g., take a very, very long time) are being broken by her and she thinks she is wrong.

This is what we do to our youth. We try to put doubt in their minds and make them old. Fortunately she is only partly-listening to the old ways of how long it takes the world to get better, because she arrives at the correct place, a painting class.

Who would say that the most important skill for creating peace in the world is painting? Not only do we need to believe that change can happen much faster than we thought, we also can believe that creativity as represented to her by painting is what is needed to change the old ways of separation and distance and things taking a long time.

"There was a big group of people and we were all waiting for the class to start. I was talking to this guy beside me and we became really good friends. The instructor started off with a dance routine with only half the people. They were dancing a certain dance in a circle. Then I was next to come and join. I still had a paintbrush in my hand with yellow paint on it, wondering what this has to do with painting, but went along with it anyways. The instructor showed me the exact steps really quickly and I was supposed to know them perfectly and do them with everyone else . . ."

Creativity requires that you have a certain openness to new ideas and new inspirations. If the old ways were good enough, they would have already worked. If we truly wish to change the world and make it united, then we can allow creativity to take its rightful place. The old ways don't work because they don't take into account that it is possible to acquire new skills and virtues that mankind has never seen before. She starts off with making friends with a person next to her. This is really the key of all the keys to peace and she already knows how to do it. If we could just make friends with the person beside us we would have peace very quickly, but look at all of the religions, nations, tribes, races who can not just make friends very quickly like young people can. She can do it and the next part of the dream tells how she extends the practice much more quickly. She is being instructed by her painting teacher to dance. This is because dance is based upon following a sequence of steps in a rhythm. Since she already knows how to make friends, all she needs to do now is to enter into the rhythm of doing it. The dream is telling us that we need to make a creative leap forward by making friends with those beside us and then entering into a rhythm of doing it.

The dream ends with her taking a creative leap of faith without knowing exactly why or what relationship it has to the ultimate ends. The only reason she doesn't know why is that most of us think that peace comes from governments having peace talks. We don't know the power of friendships in creating a united world because it seems so small and insignificant in comparison to a highly publicized peace negotiation of famous leaders.

If I were to sum the lesson of the dream in one sentence, I would say that it is telling us to dance to the beat of friendship—making with lots of enthusiasm, and then change will happen quickly.

Questions and Exercises upon which to meditate

1. Think about the part of you that you think is the hardest to change and probably have been told that you can't change. Write it in a journal. (e.g. timidity, out of control temper, can't finish what you start, being taken advantage of)

   Do one thing today that is exactly the opposite of the hardest thing to change. It can be very simple.

   Examples of opposition:

   a. "I am really shy about meeting new people." (holding back around having to interact around new people) The issue is centered around the possibility of some sort of rejection when new people are around.

   Activity: Do something simple that you have never done before like going bowling. Count the number of

people you have to talk to that you never knew before.
Then risk little things like asking for a different pair of
shoes. Go to a new place to eat each day for lunch.

b. "I get really mad when people cut me off in traffic."
    (this is because you cut yourself off when you are right
    in the midst of wonderful change process)

    Activity sample: Do something that you normally
    quit (cut yourself off) in the middle, but this time
    extend it beyond your normal amount. For instance,
    if you run for 20 minutes normally, extend it to 25 or
    30. Keep gradually extending.

c. "I am really uncomfortable to go out walking because
    I was robbed." (take away the activity you like to do
    because someone else is a thief)

    Activity sample: Find a place where you love to walk
    and walk there at your favorite time when conditions
    are really great. (giving yourself what you love to do)
    Do something you love to do each day where you feel
    comfortable and safe.

d. "I get really nervous that things won't go right so I criticize
    people around to get things perfect." (criticizing and
    tensing in order to reach a high standard)

    Activity sample: Do something where you have to
    make lots of mistakes in order to improve (something
    that requires accuracy). Keep track of your improvement
    and how you make improvements. Notice when you
    improve, that criticism and tensing has absolutely
    nothing to do with improvement. Improvement comes
    from relaxing and finding the right strategies and then
    repeating them.

e. "I start an innovative project and it has some flaws,
    but it is making steady progress. My supervisor
    criticizes the mistakes and makes me go back to the
    old ways. I get furious."

    Activity sample: Go to the supervisor and ask him
    to tell you all of the positives about the project and

then recommend a solution to the flaws. Then ask him for a rationale for the solution. Ask him everyday for feedback that is positive and solution oriented.

Each day for 15 days repeat the activity until it becomes a habit.

2. Start saying hello to people in public places that you don't know. Develop the habit of starting friendships by greeting people and starting a conversation.

3. How would your life be different if you believed you could change much faster than you believe now? Write a few sentences or even a paragraph on how it would be different.

Summary of some of symbols

Train—straight path, single minded, going somewhere on a direct path without choices
Dancing—movement which has as its purpose the creation of joy,
Paintbrush—expressiveness

Commonality of symbols

Each of the above symbols represent a type of movement—first the dreamer is not in control of the movement, then the dreamer uses her own feet but it is directed by another, and finally the dreamer is controlling the movements with her own hand. The dream goes from less control of movement to more control and from no expression to total expression.

CHAPTER 2

TAKING A WILD RIDE

Shedding the Old and Becoming an Adventurer

"I am in a car with Mom and Family. She is driving and gets into an accident. She is all shook up so I volunteer to drive. I am driving (YES! I am finally driving!). The road turns into a weird curvy tunnel like a skate board park. It is very adventurous, then we get rid of the car because the tunnel is too small and dangerous. Now we are on a big skate board going through this really wavy tunnel. We then go onto a golf course and then into a mall. Now we have no car. The car is way up on the hill. We stay in the city and go up to the university which is filled with amazing light and color and people. We then end up in a comic book store and keep coming in and out, in and out. There's a whale, maybe I am riding it. I buy a 1-cent candy and the guy messes up and gives me too much money back. So I give him the right amount back and he hugs me and kisses my cheek."

This dream is better understood in context with the previous dream. Just as your daily life is connected one day to the next, so is your dream life. It is very helpful for me to hear people's dreams over the course of a few days or weeks because then I can track the progress of their lives. In the first dream she started in the waking life last in relationship to me. In this dream she is last in relationship to her mother. This means that she is still allowing her mother to lead although she really needs to lead. It is only when her mother gets into an accident that she is allowed to drive.

Everything in a dream is told in symbolic language. Understanding symbols is what allows you to gain meaning from a dream. For instance, a car in the real world is a form of taking you from one place to another, a means of transportation. It is different than a train in that you usually have more control over how you are going to get there and how much time you are going to take. A train has a single track, but a car can get to more specific places easier. Whoever is driving the car is in control of the situation.

In a symbolic sense driving means getting from one part of your life to the next or developing a part of yourself. When you are a passenger in a dream, it means that you are not in full control of your life. When you are a passenger in a real car, you do not have much control over where the car is going. In a dream, when young people start taking over the controls of the car, they usually have inside of themselves the controls that their mothers have had over them. In order to live your own life, you have to take over control from your mother. This is because each person is created uniquely and has the responsibility of overcoming the weaknesses of the previous generation. If, at some point in your life, you do not seize control over your own life, then the civilization does not have a way of moving forward. In this dream the mother gets into an accident and then the daughter takes over. This is because after the mother has done her job as mother, the daughter already potentially has the solutions for the future inside of her. It is not the previous generation that has the solutions for the future, it is the younger generation. An accident in real life is a mistake that is often caused by carelessness or by extending the limits of one's abilities beyond what is safe. Mothers can only guide children to a certain point, then they have to let go and let the children control their own lives and believe that their children actually have something to offer them. However, accidents happen at this point when mothers keep control (driving) beyond their appointed times. It is not that the real mother is controlling beyond her appointed time in this dream, but the daughter is learning how to take control of her own self. The size of the crash depends largely on the degree to which mothers are unwilling to let go of control. Fortunately, in this dream the crash is not very severe, which means that the mother's hold on the daughter wasn't that great.

In the next part of the dream, the journey (after she takes control) turns adventurous and all of the symbols point to a ride that is less certain and more risky. Once again it indicates the necessity to have a youthful, adventurous spirit in order to deal with much of the unpredictability of the road ahead. It also takes much flexibility and resourcefulness which are qualities often available in large quantities with youth. It shows us that, like the first dream, the energy of the youth is better for making the necessary changes to the world. This does not mean that we want to throw out the energy of wisdom and past knowledge when we want to change something, but that we don't want to start out with it. After all, we have never had a condition of world peace so we really don't have an experience in our collective memories that would lead us there.

In the first dream she started on a train and end in a class. In this dream she is in a car and finds another place of learning, a university filled with amazing light and color and people, but it comes after the demonstration of an adventurous spirit. This tells us that learning is preceded by enthusiasm and adventure and not the other way around. We are enlightened after we have an adventurous attitude. Enthusiasm is a precondition for enlightenment. Finally she goes to a comic store, goes in and out, and in the end displays honesty that is greatly rewarded. She is showing us that if we have a light, humorous attitude on top of adventure then it will be easy for us to be honest with ourselves and others which will allow amazing things to happen. Honesty is often fostered best in a really light atmosphere rather than an environment heavy with judgment.

So this dream tells to shed the old controlling ways and take on an adventurous spirit, so that enlightenment and truth can be unfolded in a non-judgmental environment.

Questions and Exercises upon which to Meditate

1. How is your life being controlled by someone else other than yourself?
2. What energy would be released inside of you if you let the controlling part go?
3. Write down 5 things about yourself that are really weak and then laugh about them.
4. What new things would you study if you were enthusiastic?

Summary of symbols

Car with other driving—someone else in control of the movement
Accident—chance to change the locus of control
Mother—past control
Skate board park—movement that requires more skill to control than a car and requires more risk taking
Tunnel—narrowing of movement-
University—a place of enlightenment
Comic book store—place of lightness and laughter
Mistaken change—chance to be honest and create trust
Whale—lessen is bigger than you think

Commonality of symbols

Like the other dream the symbols involve movement from less control to greater control, but also the need for mistakes and accidents so that learning and change can take place.

CHAPTER 3

MOVING OUT OF THE
SHALLOW WATERS OF THE PAST

Relating to the Whole World with Depth

"I was with 3 close friends and a few other people and we were all getting packed and ready to go on a trip. We left the house and got onto long canoe-like boats that we moved with long poles pushing along the bottom of a shallow river. Suddenly we were inside a deep maze of ancient, covered canals. The water beneath us had turned into deep red blood and I started to get a little bit scared. There were human bones left out everywhere and ancient tools and pottery. We went through a part of the maze where people were shooting at us and trying to get us out of there because they wanted to steal the ancient pottery. Then we reached a part that had been turned into a museum. Here we walked through the corridors, and suddenly the person that I was with could not move their legs, they could only slide themselves with their arms across the floor. Then suddenly I was in a plane and on my way to Brazil. I could see the entire planet from above and it was all yellow, pink, and green, and it seemed to be radiating sunlight and music from the direction of Brazil."

Dreams tend to have two types of messages: positive and negative. Some dreams are mostly or entirely positive. You simply have to understand their meaning and then practice it in your life. Other dreams are primarily negative, which requires a lot of personal work to transform the messages into something positive. The dream above has a combination of positive and negative symbols. This means that you can work on the negative parts, seek to understand the positive parts, and then put the two together.

This is another dream based on the symbols of journeying. We can say that achieving peace in the world is a journey. Many people think that peace is one specific event, such as the end of war, or that peace is going to come with one miraculous change, such as a new world descending from the clouds. In this dream, peace is understood as a continuous journey that takes us through many obstacles and challenges, both to undo misdeeds of the past and to create new realities. Unlike the other two dreams, this journey starts in water and then ends in the air. In the first two dreams we traveled on the ground. In dreams, water is a fluid element with lots of give and take, like the qualities that make a relationship work. In this dream the group is traveling in canoe-like boats because they are traveling through shallow water. The shallow water represents the shallowness of the relationships of the past. The water-way turns into covered canals and then becomes a maze. A maze represents a puzzle to be solved. The first clue of the maze is the blood and dead bones and people trying to kill the travelers. The dream seems to tell us that the old ways of relating, relating in shallowness, only bring death. Even though the dream is negative in nature and contains a certain amount of fear, the experience for the young people is instructive and valuable. They find that everything about the shallowness of the past prevents them from moving forward in these days when peace in the world is so necessary. The person in the museum can only move with arms rather than feet and legs, indicating that shallow relationships keep you moving slowly in the past and do not bring you into the future.

You need deep, profound relationships, because depth of relating brings life. Young people in the path of peace in the world always have to face shallow past waters. Shallow relationships are those that are based on things that are temporary in nature, such as amassing power and wealth. They don't last. Profound relationships endure because they are based on real virtues. If the world is going to move from conflict to peace, it needs to focus on the quality of relationships that exist between people.

What is really interesting in this dream is what happens after the journey through shallow waters. She ends up flying in an airplane seeing light emanating from Brazil. Being in the air and looking at everything all at once gives you a kind of perspective that you don't get from being in the middle of things. This dream is saying that once you figure out what is needed, the next step is to gain perspective, so that you can see where to start and where to go for it.

The first emanation of light is Brazil. Why Brazil? Brazil is a country of light-hearted people. The culture is characterized by friendliness and warmth. It is difficult to find people who are not friendly in Brazil. The most amazing thing can happen in a Brazilian soccer game with local people. You can be playing a very competitive match, and people can be yelling at each other and complaining about each other's poor play, but at the end of the match everyone is completely friendly again as if none of the complaining and yelling occurred. It is a mystery to me how this happens, but people keep playing together and working together day after day and year after year.

My experience in North America is that after a game where that kind of complaining would occur many relationships would be over and you wouldn't be playing with those people any more because of the hurt and anger. In Brazil, people seem to be able to let it go instantly and then can't wait for the game next week. Even a player who doesn't have great ball control skills is invited back each week and not left out, because Brazilians prefer friendliness over taking offense.

A profound relationship will endure. It is like a journey that we look forward to often. In this dream, the step that we need to take is the step of having a friendly attitude toward the whole world—reach out to others and getting out of the shallow relationships of the past that only bring despair.

Questions upon which to meditate

1. What kinds of past hurt am I holding onto that keep me from entering into positive relationships? How have I been hurt in the past by others? How does that make me not want to enter new relationships?
2. Do I justify not relating to others because of their inadequacies?
3. Find a person who has given you reason to take offense in the past. Say something kind or positive to that person and see if they change.
4. Make a list of people, groups, or countries with whom your community or culture thinks you shouldn't be friendly because of their "poor" qualities. Make an effort to establish positive communication with someone in that group.
5. Do I allow shallow goals overcome my life?

Summary of symbols used

Canoe in shallow water—a journey of relational work that starts in meaningless relationships

Maze—puzzle to understand, a problem to solve

Blood, bones—in this case, death and destruction from shallow relationships

Walking through the museum—a journey through the past

Ancient pottery—tools and skills people used to use

Person walking by pushing himself with hands—in this case, the handicap of using the old ineffective ways

Brazil—a country where relationships are important rather than superficial

Colors and light—the result of focusing positive energy on relationships

Commonality of symbols

This dream combines movement with a consequence, showing how movement in shallowness and old ways doesn't work and how movement in positive relationships brings light and energy everywhere.

CHAPTER 4

THE EARTH IS ONE COUNTRY

Seeing Similarities in All Things

"A close friend and I were in a grocery store in a different country. It was mostly a natural foods store with a lot of vegetables. We went up to the line to pay, and she went through very quickly. When it was finally my turn to pay, the cashier got up and said he'd be right back, but he was gone for a long, long time. I started sorting out my money. I had a purse full of loose change from many different countries, but I couldn't find the right money for the country that we were in. When the cashier finally came back, he had moved my items to a new line and was starting to check them through. I was caught up trying to sort out my money though. Then I realized that while he was gone most of my money had vanished. Somebody told me that two big Korean men were just leaving the store and he thought that they had taken the money."

Dreams seem illogical and unbelievable when we think about them as representing the real world. However, they make a great deal of sense when we think about them as metaphors. Many people are overly concerned about the "real world" content of their dreams, because they are not used to thinking in metaphors. In dream work, it isn't important whether or not something will happen to you in the real world. What it is important is that you understand the message and begin to do something about it. By having the discipline to stay in the realm of metaphors, you can come up with really beautiful messages and solutions. My experience is that people who have grown up in a more technological modern world have a tendency to stop using metaphoric thinking. They think that a lot of their dreams don't mean anything because they find their dreams confusing. Dreams are best understood as metaphoric messages. As you learn how to decipher the metaphor, you can benefit a lot from "interpreting" your dreams.

The two primary symbols in this dream are food and money. Food in the physical world is the thing that fuels your body so that you can function at peak energy. Natural food gives you more energy than processed food, and vegetables are considered to be the most important food group for good health. So in this dream we are shopping for high energy. In the non-material world we get energy from positive qualities such as love, courage, honesty, forgiveness, and determination. Since we are shopping in a different country, it can mean that we are going for the development of a new part of ourselves that we haven't developed before, or it might mean that we are facing challenges that are different than the ones we have faced before. We seem to know in this dream that we need to be fortified with the best qualities at the optimal rate, but we have problems when it comes to the payment.

Money in the real world is how we pay for things. Payment is made through an exchange of material resources represented in currency. In the non-material world, we pay for the development of things with the energy of positive qualities that are expressed in positive actions.

It is important to understand some basic things about the passage of time in dreams. The wonderful thing about the dream world is that dimensions, such as the dimension of time, do not have to coincide with the real world. The real world is constrained by time running in the sequence of beginning, middle, and end, with each segment following another in sequence. In the world of dreams, the end of an event can be at the beginning of the dream, and the beginning of time can be at the end of the dream. For example, many people have the experience of remembering dreams that occurred close to their waking up. So you can simply ask yourself, "Why is the last thing you dream clearer and more easily remembered?" Why would this phenomenon occur?

In the past, it occurred to me that the last part of the dream could be the first thing I was supposed to work with, and that it was clear because it was the most important place for me to start working. Then I thought, that it might be better to start working at the end of the dream, to work through the issues from the end of the dream to the beginning. The end of the dream, the true goal, is at the beginning of the dream. When I did this, I started getting some fantastic results. Later, I discovered that the end and the beginning of the message, the dream's lesson for me, could even occur in the middle of a dream. "Dream time" does not have the limitations of the material world. When interpreting a negative dream, it seems best to proceed systematically, from the end of the dream to the beginning. In positive dreams, proceeding systematically doesn't seem as important, because positive qualities automatically function in an integrated, harmonized way. Negative dreams require solutions, and solutions require working systematically with a disciplined mind.

Another technique I use is to flip the negative energy over to its positive opposite. The solution to any negative issue is its positive opposite. When working through a negative dream, I start from the end in a disciplined fashion and keep flipping the negatives to positives until the solution reveals itself. This requires discipline, because it is easy to lose yourself in the dream's negative feelings and quick judgments. Negative emotions have the effect of depleting one's self-discipline. Working through them systematically, helps you to reach your desired path.

Now let us apply the principle of reversing negatives to their positive opposites—from the end of the dream to the beginning. This is the very end of the dream: "Somebody told me that two big Korean men were just leaving the store and he thought that they had taken the money."

The opposite of "thought that they had taken the money" is to be completely assured of giving out positive energy. Money is energy. A positive opposite of "somebody told me that two big Korean men were leaving the store" can be determined by knowing the meaning of the symbols. Here, "Korean" means foreign. For the dreamer, a Korean is from somewhere really far away. "Foreign" signifies different in a negative sense and "two" means double the problem. "Somebody told me" signifies second-hand knowledge and "thought that" implies some level of doubt. Therefore, what the dreamer seeks is assurance, first-hand certainty of arriving somewhere. instead of departing for a place of giving out rather than taken from and giving out double of what is already familiar rather than be taken by foreignness. The dream shows that the solution is to give out familiar, positive energy—in large quantities—with certainty. Familiar can mean "the same as". Consider the next section: "I was caught up trying to sort out my money though, and then realized that, in the time he was gone, most of it had vanished."

What it is important here is that when she was caught up in sorting, the money vanished. Sorting is a way of finding differences. When we are engaged in finding differences, we lose our positive energy. Notice also that the words "caught up trying to" are used. This signifies a lack of control. When we invert the statement to a positive meaning, it shows that there are bountiful amounts of positive energy when we consciously explore similarities. In the context of this dream, sorting is a negative pursuit. Finding similarities is a constructive one.

"When it was finally my turn to pay, the cashier got up and said he'd be right back, but was gone for a long, long time. I started sorting out my money. I had a purse full of loose change from many different countries, but I couldn't find the right money for the country that we were in. When the cashier finally came back, he had moved my items to a new line and was starting to check them through."

Again she is trying to find differences, but the person receiving the payment goes away for a long, long time. This means that when you are going to do something new or going to a new country or starting a new project, your energy is not helpful when you are focusing on finding differences. The friend goes through the line quickly, because she knows that when you go to a different country it is the same as the last country. Nothing has changed. People are the same. Money still does the same thing. We are not accepted internally and externally at the start of a new project when we look to the differences. We need to be certain that progress happens by finding and relating to the similarities. When you go for differences, you lose your energy.

This is so important that it cannot be overemphasized. It is especially important to the processes of establishing peace in the world and to realizing inner peace. When you cross a border and go into a new country, such as crossing the border from the United States into Mexico, there is a great tendency to think about how different things are. Besides economics, the language is not the same. But is the language so different? Don't Mexicans talk about the same things as Americans? The same sentiments are expressed in both languages. We are so accustomed to finding differences that we are fooled into thinking that things are very different when, actually, they are more similar than different. People who are experienced at moving from one culture to another first identify similarities and appreciate them, and then marvel at the new things they can learn.

The same perspective applies on a personal level. If we are used to studying languages and are very good at them, but then have to cross over to do mathematics, which may be new for us, the differences will become obvious unconsciously and instantly.

However, if we make a conscious effort to identify similarities first, the learning becomes much easier. For instance, both language and math use symbols to represent things. Both write the symbols in a sentence-like form. Both start with a few basic symbols and then expand them into great complexities.

When we begin something new, we tend to forget about our past strengths, to forget about the familiar, and to see the new thing as totally different. We haven't done it before, so we may feel totally weak in the face of developing the new abilities. But if we first consciously think about how the new thing is like the old things, then we can go into new experiences feeling very confident, with lots of strength. One reason we don't have peace in the world is that cultures emphasize differences rather than similarities. Prejudice exists because people are taught, often from a very young age, that the other group is different and, therefore, inferior or bad. Unity exists when we make a conscious effort to first appreciate the similarities, and then to marvel in the beauty of the diversity, but we need to make a conscious effort to identify similarities first.

Questions upon which to Meditate

1. Make a list of the ten things you most admire about your family. Find two other families and see the same qualities in them consciously, then evaluate your own energy to see if you don't feel more like relating to them to create a better world.

2. Think about another cultural group that you live close to. Ask yourself to identify the greatest similarity between that group and your own culture. Then say something about that group that is unique and beautiful. How do feel toward them and toward yourself?

3. Make a plan to visit a group who you thought was totally different than you. For instance, if you are young, visit a home for the elderly. Find all the similarities between you and the elderly, but don't quit until you have a very long list. Keep

making the list until it seems as though there is no difference whatsoever.

4. Identify an exercise that you think is very different from the one you are most accustomed to doing. While you are doing the new one, make a mental list of how similar it is to the other one.

Summary of symbols used

Natural foods—positive qualities that are nourishing for the soul
Different country—foreignness, feeling different than others
Many different coins—the belief that certain qualities are not valued
    in different places
Delay in payment—consequence of feeling different
Korean stealing—consequence of having unfamiliar feelings

Commonality of symbols

The symbols start with feeling differences and end with a negative consequence. In the first case, it causes a delay, in the second case, a theft. Nourishing is based on seeing how things are the same or their unifying commonality.

CHAPTER 5

THE VIRTUE OF AWE

Seeing the Beauty in Everything

The first dream

"I was in a car with 2 or 3 young men, who where very happy and celebrating something. I was not driving, one of the men was. We drove up a highway (only two lanes) that kept rising before us like a ribbon in a soft rolling effect. I didn't know the young men, but I was comfortable in the car."

The second dream: is as follows

"I was on the deck of a large ship, accompanied by a crowd of people. In the middle of the deck was a large, open hatch with a clear view of the ocean below. The ocean was very clear and shallow, and two men stood in the water. One was a clergyman, and the other was that delightful actor, Michael J. Fox. The clergyman seemed to be giving Fox last rites. Fox was going to die, and he wanted to end his life in the sea instead of on the land. It was very emotional and reverent somehow. The thing that sticks in my mind was the clearness of the water—I could easily see the sand and seashells below the shallow water."

This is a delightful dream. Usually when people dream about driving or traveling, they have difficulties either being in control or letting go of control. In this dream, the dreamer is allowed to be an observer. The dreamer is completely free of control issues and can just experience life fully without having to control it or manipulate it or get other people to do things.

If you have a perfectionist in your family, or in another relationship, or if you are a perfectionist, you will recognize that they are rarely satisfied with their work. They keep looking for it to be absolutely 100% perfect, but, no matter what they do, it doesn't satisfy them. At the end of every event or production they are left feeling some kind of disappointment. They are hard workers, pay great attention to detail, and generally organize people well to get things done. But they just never seem to like the results of what they do.

In the two dreams above, the dreamer is communicating the solution to perfectionism. She probably had the dream to remind her that this is her gift and that her application of the gift will have a tremendous effect on people around her. What is the gift? The gift she has is the ability to observe beauty and be awed by it—even with the process of death. She walks, talks, and lives in beauty, so everywhere she goes, people feel more relaxed, more beautiful, and more in awe of the world.

She has the ability to sit back and see what is already wonderful, as opposed to people who are just walking around looking for mistakes and trying to correct them. When such a gifted observer appears in a perfectionist's life, the perfectionist learns how to relax and feel satisfied for the first time. When a supervisor who has the virtue of wonderment works with a perfectionist, it is an excellent combination, because the positive things that the supervisor constantly sees keeps the perfectionist extremely motivated.

This is the first dream that is entirely positive. The feeling of awe is never lost in the dreamer's experience. These two dreams, being in a car with strangers and being at a funeral, would normally make people uncomfortable, but for her, the only important thing is the beauty around her. When you have dream that is completely positive throughout, it means the dream is completely free from ego, from the negative energy that normally pulls us down. There is nothing that one has to do to change a positive dream other than to study it forever. This dream will keep revealing itself to the dreamer for as long as she lives, and beyond, because it is connected completely with who she is and what she has been given to do in life.

It is both a blessing and a responsibility, both a gift and a trust, both a pure gem and an opportunity. She didn't choose the gift, nor did she do anything to earn it. The gift was always latent within her, and the fact that she is having the dream means that she now has enough maturity and development to use it. I can think of no gift that is more needed in the world in order to have a lasting peace than this positive outlook. I am completely awed by it, and I am thankful that I am related to her. Peace seems to be principally about beauty, seeing it, and being awed by it.

Once you have a dream like this, you can be assured that you will be asked to use it. You can't be given a great gift and then not be expected to use it constantly. The test for her will be to hold on to it and to keep doing it, even though the world is acting completely contrary to her energy. If we only had more people with this gift, I am sure the world would change instantly.

The dreams have two other interesting parts that are worth investigating. One is the road rising softly before her like a ribbon, and the other is the clearness of the water. The first is a symbol meaning that things will only get better if she stays on the same road. The second one means that when she is experiencing awe and wonder, things become very clear and she will know what to do. Water is a relational element because of its fluidity; seeing clear water means that what to do in a relationship will always be clear to her if she stays in awe.

The other really interesting thing to me is that there is nothing negative. Most of us have been told through our cultural experience that being critical and finding negatives is the way to make things better, to establish peace. This dream shows the fallacy of that thinking, because being critical is not necessary for her to do her work. She only needs to see the positive and act upon it.

Questions/Experiences for Reflection

1. Find out what you do already that is successful. Either analyze yourself or ask a friend or co-worker to tell you ways you are successful. Make sure you go into detail and make the analysis at least one page long.
2. Take a beauty walk. Practice finding beauty in things you see, and acknowledge them by being amazed at what you see. An American Aboriginal friend once told me that everything in nature loves to be acknowledged.
3. Go to an area that has a lot of poverty and start looking around for things that are beautiful, like the way people are talking to each other, their smiles, or their hospitality.
4. Remember a bad experience where you felt really negative. Analyze the experience closely until you find something positive. Keep analyzing the positive and exaggerating it until you realize that the positive part of the experience was really important and worth remembering.

Summary of symbols used

Being a comfortable passenger in a car—letting go of ego control
A highway that rises like a softly-rolling ribbon—a path of
    wonderment and perception
Large ship with a crowd—a way to observe aspects of other people
Shallow, clear water—being clear about people's behavior
Observing death—the ability to see all aspects of life, including
    death

Commonality of symbols

The dreamer is a passenger and an observer. It demonstrates the ease of letting go and letting others direct the trip, while she observes and learns through observation of the wonders of life in all its aspects.

CHAPTER 6

RETIREMENT BLUES

Life Doesn't End When You Retire

"I have had recurring dreams that instead of retiring from the school district, I stayed on and worked. Also, I never was the Principal, so I carried on as an assistant or as a teacher. I found that I never checked my mailbox at school as I signed in, and I often would find a stack of bulletins a few days later. This was very real and embarrassing in the dreams."

"Another recurring dream through the years had me teaching swimming to my night adult classes. It happened again two nights ago as I was teaching a beginner class. I became aware of the dream as I was awakening, and I didn't want it to end, so I played it out for some time to make sure that the lesson was completed."

The wonderful thing about this dream is that it shows that even though a person retires from a profession, life still goes on. People who have retired have a great advantage over younger people, because they have more freedom and a lifetime full of experience upon which to draw. What tends to happen at the retirement age is that people attend to things that they had deferred dealing with.

Recurring dreams mean that the issue is persistent; you haven't yet made enough progress on it to move on. If you have worked on a recurring dream, it will either go away or will change. If you don't work with it, it will tend to get worse with time. A recurring dream really has to be attended to. In the above cases, the first one is negative and the second one is positive.

The second dream suggests that the dreamer takes a lot of responsibility to complete what he starts, especially when it comes to teaching others. He stays with it, even repeatedly, to make sure that the goals are accomplished. This demonstrates that he is dependable. We can count on him; he will be always be there. He fulfills the commitments he makes. The whims of politics do not affect this type of person. They are in it for the long haul; they don't stop until the job is completed.

In the first dream, he encounters problems. Instead of retiring, he is faced with a recurring problem that becomes embarrassing. In the dream, he is dealing with mail. Before he was a principal, he always had to deal with receiving communication from other people. This was never dealt with to his satisfaction. He feels embarrassed that he can't answer everyone's demands. He doesn't understand that he has a lot to communicate to others.

In the second dream, he is committed to doing good work. He is reluctant, even embarrassed, to share it with others because he knows that the best work is done by deeds and not with words. He is reluctant to speak because he knows that words can actually detract from performance. However, as an administrator, when it is his turn to communicate, he thinks that words are really important. This is why he is embarrassed. He was competent in a world of action, but he doesn't feel that he makes a competent administrator.

Now retired, he still has the issue because he is still dreaming about it. If it were not possible for him to solve it in his current life, he wouldn't have had the dream. This means that he still can deal with the issue of communication and the embarrassment surrounding it. How does he solve it? The way he solves it is by understanding what an administrator does and how communication serves the community in which he is serving. Administrators often see themselves as high up on the ladder and consider the workers as below them. Communication often is seen as a way that the higher-ups can tell the lower-downs what to do. As the purpose of communication is to make a connection between one person and another, it is best done when there is a sense of equality in the communication. This is because relationships that are based upon equality work better than those that are based upon dominance. Human beings are not naturally designed to dominate each other. Most hierarchical methods of administration are out of touch with human nature. We are designed naturally to connect intimately with each other, and we can do so only when there is equality.

In the second dream, the dreamer shows that he is very connected to his students. He goes back to see that they accomplished everything because he has a great desire for them to succeed. The dreamer wants to be a successful administrator. In real life, he has already found out how to do this, but he hasn't achieved it yet. In his real life he writes newsletters for his alumni groups. Why does this make him successful as an administrator? He is serving a community of individuals who attended the same school. Through collecting and publishing their current stories, he keeps them connected and in relationship with each other. When he was an administrator, he probably did the same thing. There was a lot of harmony and peace in his schools. However, because of the nature of hierarchy and power, he didn't think he fulfilled the role of an administrator. But nearly everyone who worked with him really liked him. They were extremely grateful for the privilege of serving in a school where he was principal. His method is really very simple and if other administrators would use it they would have great results.

Keep everyone connected by telling their stories to others.

Questions and Activities for Reflection

1. Listen to some good news about what someone did and then tell it to 5 other people. As you tell it, watch how their faces brighten.
2. Read through some of the communication you are getting from an administrative source. Ask yourself if they are just

trying to get something from you or are they sincerely trying to keep you connected? If they are trying to keep you connected, affirm your good fortune and your gratitude.

3. Make a list a people from your past with whom you wish you could somehow be reconnected. and then use my father's method and it won't be long until you find them.

4. What part of your inner self are you missing? Think back to a time when you felt well-connected to that part Determine how you could re-establish a connection with it.

Example: The part of you that exercises a lot and loves to play sports. The last time you really consistently exercised was in high school. When you entered university, you stopped because university requires much more self motivation rather than the culture of sports in high school. You could write a little note like this:

> Dear athletic guy,
> It has been a long time since I last saw you, too long I think. I was remembering when I used to see you everyday and how great it was especially the feelings after a game or a good workout. I hear that you play in volleyball league a couple of times per week and then do some swimming on other days. I have been thinking about joining you. Is it still possible?
>
> Mr. Outtashape

> Dear Outta,
> Wow what a surprise to get your letter! It would be great if you could join the activities. Nowadays I usually start with a lot of stretching and today I am going to see my cardiologist to make sure everything is working. I'll make an appointment with you if you like.
>
> See you there
> Alwaysmoving

Summary of Symbols Used

Stack of unread mail—not being able to feel connected with others
Didn't retire from school—continuation of old issue
Didn't become Principal—feeling that he didn't do a good job as
    Principal
Teaching swimming—teaching people how to connect
Returning to see that the job is completed—a great desire to see
    people connected

Commonality of Symbols

The major commonality is the desire to have people feel connected and unified, so that they act as one community and thus get the work done better.

CHAPTER 7

THE FLYING TEDDY BEAR

When Being Strong Means Being Gentle

"I dreamt that I was on a mountain. There were other people there, but I didn't know them. I think I was attending a summer school or camp. A young man in his twenties was going to guide us down the mountain to the water. I wanted to get to know him, but he didn't want to talk to me, it seemed, because of my age (47). So I walked ahead on the path. As it wound down the mountain, I decided to fly. There were many people on the path, and I flew over their heads then landed lightly, walked a bit, and then flew again, this time landing on the trail almost at the bottom. I started walking and came upon a gigantic stuffed bear. I walked around to his front and noticed his foot moving, and realized he was alive. I said to someone, "He's alive!"

Then he stood up beside me; he was just a little bigger than me. We started talking and walking, and I held his paw. I felt very close to him. I marveled that he could speak English and that he was so gentle and human-like. He said he would like to come to Brazil and wanted to know if it were possible. I looked at him carefully to see if he would fit in an airplane seat. I decided that he was about the size of an overweight human and told him I thought he would fit. (There were a lot of people around this field, and they didn't notice him, which surprised me.)

Then I woke up."

This dream starts on the top of a mountain. This is an unusual place to start; usually, people start at the bottom and work their way up, but not this dreamer. Mountains often represent challenges; to get to the top of a mountain, you have to undergo great difficulty and hardship. She is already there. This means that she already has overcome the challenges of getting here and now she is on top. In most societies, the methods of administration have been invented primarily by men. Often, we encounter a scratching and clawing to get to the top. Some people regard it a great accomplishment to be the president of a company or to be the one responsible for the final decision. In contrast, top and bottom do not have that kind of importance for women. A man's ambition might be to stay on the top of the mountain, but this dreamer's ambition is to get down to the water. Why is this important?

When you are "on top", you might regard yourself as important and great; you might have the illusion that you can do whatever you want and that you have the power to control everything. Furthermore, a company's success is often attributed to the top person. An organization is only as good as the strong qualities of the entire work force, the way they interact with each other, and the way they respond to challenges. If the top person understands that he is only as good as the people "below" him, he has a chance of running a successful organization. Women usually understand that power is based upon the quality of the interactions they have with other people, not merely the title or rank they may have in the organization. This is why they are better peacemakers. The title isn't as important as the way the group interacts with each other. The goal for women is usually harmony, in contrast with men's training to focus upon individual achievement.

In her dream, the goal of the dreamer is to get to the water at the bottom. Water is a relational element; it is fluid and dynamic. To be successful, relationships must move like water. Her goal is not to be on top, but to get to the bottom, so that the top will come down to an equal level. If you have water on a mountain, it only has one choice—to flow down the mountain to the lake. The mountain water does not flow up to the top. If you want the blessings of the water (relationships) to come to you, the best place to be is at the bottom. The bottom is the place of greatest equality, harmony, and humility.

In the dream, she is in a school that is being led by a 20-year-old man. In order to learn, a person needs the quality of humility. Like a lake at the bottom of a mountain, you take the position of greatest receptivity when you lower yourself. This is not to be confused with humiliation, which is the process of being subjected to mistreatment or abuse. Humility is the quality of being receptive. This is the dreamer's goal. Unfortunately, she runs into an arrogant 20-year-old man, a person full of himself, who thinks he knows it all and can ignore the wisdom and experience of a woman more than twice his age. The way she passes through arrogance is impressive. Not many people can leave an arrogant man so easily behind, but she handles it with ease.

The next part of the dream is incredible; she decides to fly and she does! Flying is an upward movement that goes against the law of gravity. Not only is she moving toward receptivity, now she is going *up* to get *down*. This is an interesting paradox. She is not flying up to get higher; she is flying up to get down—because for her, down is up and up is down. Down is the place of the greatest receptivity. So, to feel really "up", to be "on top", she wants to leave the place of greatest arrogance. Therefore, up is down and down is up. She can leave the earth's gravity because she has abandoned one of the society's archaic doctrines; she has begun to travel in unfamiliar, non-material dimensions.

It is difficult for men in dominant Western cultures to understand that up can be down and down can be up, because principles like equality and humility are dismissed when scratching for the top. People from other cultures readily hear it in the language. For example, in Afro-American street culture, when something is called "bad", it is really good. In their experience, as in much of women's culture, a white man in authority, such as a police officer, supposedly represents the good values. Often however, when a white police officer charges a black person with supposedly doing something bad, the police officer is seen as being the one doing the bad thing. In this perspective, the "good" person behaved badly, and the one who was charged with being bad was innocent, "good." When "street people" call a person bad, they mean he is good. A person identified as "bad" in a white person's eyes might be considered "good" in a black person's eyes.

In the realm where the dreamer is going, language is reversed. Terminology ceases to have its literal meaning and shifts to the exact opposite. The people who really seem to understand this concept are the ones who aren't clawing their way to top, who don't acquiesce to titles and positions and the traditional hierarchy. When your focus is on getting to the water, you understand that "near" can mean far, and that "young" can be old. In many dominant cultures, institutions do not seem to concern themselves with relationships. Wars and conflicts over who should be on top of the mountain continue to exist in the world. But our dreamer has flown above the struggle for dominance, "the top". She moves quickly to what is open for her in the world of opposites at "the bottom". She is giving us a lesson in world peace and letting us know how to move there rapidly.

When her feet are back on the solid ground, she encounters a highly unlikely creature, a gigantic stuffed bear that comes to life. Having her feet solidly on the ground is a symbol that tells us she is not in the world of illusions, she is not floating in clouds of imagination. She is paying solid, firm attention, even though what she sees seems to be an illusion. In this part of the dream, imagination is real and what seems to be real is imagination. By applying the concept that up can be down and down can be up, we understand that the stuffed bear is real. That others don't see the bear indicates that they are that the understanding of who the bear is remains in their imagination because the qualities of the bear are not yet realized for them.

A bear is an animal that is strong and powerful. When we think of a bear, we think of a powerful animal. It is interesting that when we make teddy bears for children, we use one of the most powerful animals to portray the quality of gentleness. We portray one of the strongest animals in the world of nature as being gentle in the world of children. Why did the teddy bear appear?

It shows us that gentleness is one of the most powerful virtues we possess. The teddy bear is just like the water. It moves gently, humbly over the land moving toward its goal. Water is not rigid and dense, it takes the shape of the object it is passing over and moves gently through it. In the dream, she can't take a lake with her, but she can take the teddy bear. Both represent the same wonderful quality, gentleness; it is difficult to imagine a quality that brings greater peace to people. Gentleness does not mean weakness; we have the example of the Grand Canyon to prove water's power.

The power of gentleness is the power to make room for other people's faults and failings so that the real person can come out. People who have lots of friends, like the dreamer, make room for other people's faults. They don't exclude a person or judge them as bad for their weaknesses. They make room for other people, because they know that we all have many faults and weaknesses. If we were all to sit in judgment of each other, which many of us do, we would be really lonely in the world. True peace is about making lots of friends and then being really gentle with them. We owe a lot to this dreamer, for she has shared a great lesson with us.

Questions for Meditation

1. Think of a person with whom you are having a very difficult relationship. See if you can identify a weakness that the other person is showing. Next, identify a weakness of yours that might be hampering your relationship with that person. Is

there a way for you to make more room for each other's weaknesses so that you can be friends?

2. Practice the skill of opposites by answering some of these challenges.

    —When can a weakness be a strength?
    —When is being a ravenous wolf a positive quality?
    —When is stealing really giving? (Not Robin Hood!)
    —When is giving really taking?

3. Think of a few examples in your life when someone was really gentle with you and it helped you.

4. Think about the way your organization is designed, and see if you can find ways that friendships can be fostered more readily, so that you can benefit from other people's knowledge and wisdom. If you want to break down a rigidly hierarchical place of work, practice the simple exercise of talking to people in different levels. If you are administrator, make conversation with cleaning staff.

Summary of symbols used

the top of the mountain—having reached a goal, feeling on top of
     things, feeling good about yourself
water—gentleness
20-year-old man—arrogance
flying—ease of action
water below—humility, gentleness, equal relationships
giant teddy bear—gentleness

Commonality of symbols

The symbols show that gentleness is a powerful quality that you can use when dealing directly with other people. This experience can feel really good!

CHAPTER 8

WHAT'S BUGGING YOU

What is Under the Surface?

"I looked down at my feet and there were all these little bugs crawling and squiggling around inside my skin in the bottoms of my feet. I freaked out and wanted to take a knife and cut open my feet to get them out, but if I did, they would go into my blood stream and then lay eggs. It was really scary. At the same time, I was walking on the bare earth and trying to get away from some teenage guys who were chasing us through this big tunnel in the earth. There were a few other girls with me but I lost them. When we got to the end, I was safe but I still had the bugs in my feet."

Sometimes the metaphors are so apparent in a dream that you need little time to think about them. The most common metaphors are familiar expressions and often are cultural universals, that is, they are found in nearly every culture. In communities where there are many bugs, people are likely to have this kind of dream. All you have to do is ask the person, "What is bugging you?"

In this dream, what is bugging her is pretty intense, because she wants to take a knife and cut it out. However, she realizes that cutting out the thing that is bugging her just makes it worse. Fortunately, in the dream we can see that what is bugging her are teenage boys chasing after her in a tunnel. Since she doesn't know the boys, we can assume that she has a problem with boys who act in an "immature" way. She is trying to run away from the way teenage boys act. Running through a tunnel means that she perceives them as having "one-track" minds—they are trying to get her to do what they want. She gets away from them, but she loses her girl friends in the process. This young woman doesn't want to play a shallow "relationship game". She can get away from the way things are, but she is still irritated—something is still bugging her under her skin.

A person doesn't have to play the "relationship game;" it doesn't usually lead to lasting relationships. But this also can leave a person feeling lonely and not knowing what to do. What should she do?

The answer is amazingly simple, but very profound. Instead of being bugged by the culture and cutting out relationships, when she practices another way of living, meaningful relationships will show up. The way for her to do it is to be completely committed to doing what she loves to do; people who are attracted to that kind of person just show up. Regrettably, what many people try to do to establish a relationship is exactly the opposite; they spend time trying to look good for someone else. They go through all kinds of things that they don't really like to do in an attempt to be attractive to someone else. And the other person is doing the same thing, just trying to look good. Being involved in something that you really love doing is very attractive, because it gives off a lot of positive energy. When you attempt to put on a show, not to be who you really are, the energy only lasts for a short period of time.

Another interesting thing about this dream is that it involves the bottom of her feet; she is walking on the bare earth. Sometimes it is good to have your feet planted solidly on the ground and to do the reasonable thing, but, in this case, the feet are the wrong metaphor. She should do something crazy, something that no one else does, rather than trying to "be reasonable" like other people. If she goes crazy, she can have a good time and find great relationships. But, if she tries to be "grounded" like others, she will get "bugged" and start scratching until she can't stand it. Good relationships come by breaking the phony cultural patterns. It is that simple.

If we want peace in the world, we need to start looking at what has caused so much war. War doesn't begin in presidential palaces or the houses of government. War begins by everyone following the bad patterns of their forefathers, especially the ones where you are attempting to impress others. If you impress your own true self, there is no conflict, because the true self is naturally unifying and peace-loving. It finds the path of peace in relationships because it is looking for true harmony.

Questions for meditation

1. What is the thing that is bugging you the most in your life?
2. How do you let others under your skin?
3. What do you really want to do that the culture thinks is foolish or that is not in line with the way people are expected to behave?
4. Think of something that you have always wanted to do and do it.

Summary of symbols used

Bugs—things that are bothering you
Under the skin—something beneath the surface that you can't get rid of
Knife—trying to just get rid of the annoyance by getting rid of the people causing it
Boys chasing her—single-mindedness of teenage boys going after girls
Tunnel—forced down a narrow way of acting
Bare feet running—trying to be grounded

Commonality of Symbols

The symbols are about being forced down a narrow path of adolescence; being annoyed by having to do what everyone else does. The goal is to be independent, to do the opposite of others and to discover extraordinary relationships.

CHAPTER 9

BEING IN THE WRONG PLACE
AT THE RIGHT TIME

"It started out like I was going tree planting. I had brought all my stuff and we were finding places to camp. We were sitting on a really big mountain; all of a sudden it started sinking (like there was an earthquake or something) and it was sliding into water. We all started running for higher ground. We all made it, but our stuff all disappeared into the deep water below. Then we found out that one of the foremen was going crazy and trying to kill everyone. Then bloody people came out of their cabins screaming, and the foreman was after us. I locked myself into a room and gathered ceramic pots and pepper spray to use as weapons if he broke the door down."

"After that trauma was all over, I was with my sister, and I was looking through some paintings she had done. Then I realized that the paintings were actually of places I had been to before that were now underwater. But she had painted them a long time ago, and my dad was going to write a book that went along with them. Then I was practicing capoeira*. I had to go to the bathroom, so I was walking down the hallway, but I noticed that I wasn't wearing any pants, so I went looking for them. I passed the mestre* of the capoeira studio that I go to here, and he giggled and then gave me

---

*   Capoeira is Brazilian form of martial arts that was created as a dance and martial during the times of slavery. A mestre is the person who leads the capoeira class or group and a roda is Portuguese for circle because in capoeira everyone sits or stands in circle while people are performing.

five. Then I looked down and noticed that I was holding my pants in my hand, so I quickly put them on. Then I saw one of my really close friends talking to someone seriously, and she walked by me. I ran back to the Roda* (circle of capoeira) to play with everyone."

The locations are the most significant parts of this dream. Two realities that we always have to deal with in life are time and space. In this dream, space is much more important than time. If the dreamer will change the spatial dimensions of the negatives, she will find that everything will work out. The first interesting thing that happens is that a mountain sinks while they are sitting on top of it. The question to ask is, "What is a sinking mountain?" Mountains usually represent challenges, but when you are sitting on top of a mountain, you have vision. In Native American culture, the most sacred place for a tribe was often the highest point, because it is from the highest point that you can see the furthest; from this point you can contemplate what action to take in the future. In the dream, they are sitting on a mountain top (contemplating the future action) and it begins to sink, and then they lose all of their stuff in the water.

At this point, I want to ask the question, "Why, at this moment in time, is the mountain top the wrong place?" The obvious answer is that it is sinking. The next question is, "Why is it sinking?" The reason is that when you are tree planting, a forest activity, you don't need vision, you just need lots of action. The future is not what is important. The important thing is the immediate activity, and lots of it. The equipment sinks into the water and then the foreman goes mad, because the dreamer is too busy contemplating the future and not doing anything in the present that will insure a future. Instead of doing lots of things that insures a future, she locks herself in the room or sits on a mountain top contemplating and gets nothing done. This is not to say that meditation on a mountain and seeking vision are not important activities. They are extremely important, but they are the wrong place (activity) at the right time. She simply has to stop sitting and get into action and everything will be solved. There is a time for sitting and a time for acting, and this one is a time for acting. The right place is in the forest. The second half of the dream shifts from the future tense to the past tense. She is looking through a series of images that have already been painted, a history of paintings before the sinking. This means that there is something important for her to remember about where she had been before the sinking. The best way to get out of trauma is to start in the past, before the trauma, and to remember positive things that have already occurred. Remembering is a process that builds confidence, if you are remembering positive things. She sank into a slump because of too much contemplation and not enough action. To get out the slump and back into action, she needs to remember positive things that have already worked for her. Her sister and her father are two people who help her to get into the remembering process to regain confidence before she can face the issue at hand and take action.

Taking action is presented in the context of capoeira and going to the bathroom. Capoeira is a type of Brazilian martial art that combines gymnastic rhythmic moves with defensive martial arts moves. In a dream, going to the bathroom is a symbol for getting rid of something that you are carrying, usually some negative energy that needs releasing so that positive energy can be released. It is a natural process to have positive action released as a result of getting rid of negative energy. In many bathroom dreams, the emotion of embarrassment appears, which is what happens in this case. She doesn't have any pants at first, but when she sees her teacher, who acknowledges what has happened and lets her know that it is ok, then she finds her pants and continues with what she needs to do. The embarrassment is about entering an activity and not being sure of yourself, and being reluctant to get into things. However, once she knows that she is ok, then she can join in.

The second part of the dream is a solution for the first part. In the first part, she needed to get into action but was stuck in her meditative process. In the second part of the dream, she is taught how to do true meditation that leads to action. The steps are quite easy but often confused. Meditation or therapy often begin in a remembering process that builds self confidence and then releases a new energy to confront the issue at hand, understand it and let it go. Remembering our successes and taking confident action are necessary and inseparable if we want to have change on a continual basis, especially to overcome trauma.

Questions for Meditation

1. When and how have you ever been in the wrong place at the right time? (ex. being really ready to learn, but being in a really bad school or program)
2. What are some strengths or positive qualities that you have that always work well for you? (You don't want to lose these things when you are in the change process.)
3. What is the most important issue you are facing right now in your life?
4. What new energy would be released if you could get rid of the problem inside of you?

Summary of symbols

top of the mountain—place of contemplation
tree planting—action needs to be taken
sinking of the mountain—wrong place to be
picture in the deep water—vivid positive memories of the past
    that are very meaningful
capoeira—practicing the rhythmic qualities of life that are needed
    for action
no pants—embarrassment
bathroom—place to let go of issues, problems

Commonality of symbols

The symbols show that when you are doing the wrong thing at the right time you have problems. [The first part is being in the present by trying to be in the future. The second is being in present but needing to be in the past first.]

CHAPTER 10

HOW TO ROB YOUR SELF

Invest in Your True Self

"I was cleaning my house and organizing everything. My husband and I lived in a large apartment on the bottom floor. A friend of ours came to the door and asked if we wanted to go do laundry together, so my husband went out with her and I went back inside to get the laundry. When I was inside, I heard someone rattling our other door that led to the lobby, trying to get in. I wanted to go see who it was, but I didn't want them to see me, because I was scared that they might try to hurt me. I left the house and went to the police station to report the crime. When I was there, I saw a bum lying just outside the station, and I thought he was the same guy who tried to break into my house. I told the cops, and they immediately went back to my house to set up a huge barricade. Cops were all over the house with huge shotguns, waiting for the man to come back to the house again. I went outside for a minute, then tried to get back inside the house. It was surrounded by police and nobody would let me in; they didn't recognize me, even though I kept saying that it was my house. The closer I tried to get the house, the further away I got (the blocks seemed to increase even though I was getting closer)."

The key to understanding this dream starts with the activity at the beginning of the dream, cleaning. Cleaning means purifying. The purpose of purifying in the spiritual world is to make it easier to understand and be receptive to the guidance that comes from spirit. If you clean the dust off a mirror, you see who you are more clearly. Impurity usually means doing something for the wrong reasons, or trying to take the easy way out, or looking for material gain. It takes you off the path of who you are, and it defiles your activities and your life until you no longer recognize who you are.

The dream starts very well, because they are all cleaning. But then, in the midst of the purifying process, a thief comes into her consciousness. Immediately she becomes frightened and does the logical thing, calling the police to get protection. But instead of getting closer to what she wants, she ends up further away. The question to ask here is, "Why, if she is doing the logical protective thing, does she end up further from her house, her self?" It is difficult to persuade people who are fearful to not go for protection, especially in a dream, but that is exactly what needs to happen. She is fearful of an intruder, and she is taken further from her self when she goes for protection.

In both the material world and the spiritual world, it is important to ask yourself who the intruder is, because you can't solve the dream until you know the answer to this question. Because this is a dream about purity, you can assume that the intruder is a part of you that breaks in and takes you away from your true self. In this dream, she says that the intruder is a bum who ends up lying out close to the police station. We characterize a bum as a person who doesn't have a lot of direction and who usually takes the easy way out to get what he wants. It is when the dreamer is cleaning her house, that the intruder appears. This means a part of her wants to take the easy way to get what she wants. What makes it difficult to accept in a dream like this is that no one wants to admit that they have a part of them that wants to take the easy way out. Culturally, we are taught to have pure motives and to go for things honestly. In our present day and age, however, these moralities often are seen more like faults than virtues. Sometimes, a part of us just wishes it were easier, and that things would just come our way without doing the things we were meant to do.

However, when you have purity and leave yourself open to spiritual guidance, then who you truly are starts to appear.

When you take this dream seriously, what is even more amazing is that you stop being protective. You admit that you are not doing something that you should be doing, and you commit yourself to doing what is important for you to do. You find that the thing that opens up is the thing you love the most. To get back to being her true self, back to her home, she has to remember to do the thing she loves the most, the thing that makes her feel the most like herself. And she really needs to do it more often. An intruder or a thief is a symbol of taking the easy way out, because a thief doesn't have the faintest clue about who he is and what he should be doing.

It may seem unusual, but communities would find it very "cost-effective" to invest money in helping people find out who they are and what they enjoy doing, and then encourage them to do it often. This would be more effective than investing huge sums in protective services, because more protection doesn't bring about change.

Questions for Meditation

1. What is the one thing that I am really fearful of being honest about with myself ?
2. What kinds of things intrude into my life that take me away from things that really reflect who I am and what I was meant to do?
3. What am I protective about that I can let go of now?
4. How can I give myself over to things that I truly love?
  "Truthfulness is the foundation of all human virtues."

Summary of symbols used

laundry—process of purifying clothing (roles)
friend doing it with them—she is already friendly with herself in
  the things she does

bum who tries to break in—[part that won't accept the role she
    has to play]
police—seeking protection from an intruder
barricade—protection around self that doesn't allow self to function
distance—how close you feel to who you are

Commonality of symbols

The symbols show how protection is used when we aren't being
true to ourselves. This takes us further away from our goals.

CHAPTER 11

KILLING GODZILLA
(FIRST OF FOUR CONSECUTIVE DREAMS)

Changing a Huge Negative into Endless Positives

"In the first dream, I was in a house with my family. Godzilla came in out of nowhere and was trying to capture us. We were all very frightened and ran out of the house, all trying to get in the car, only we didn't all fit. Only the women fit in the car, so we started to drive away, watching the men try frantically to get into the other car. As we were driving away, I saw that their car wouldn't start and that Godzilla was leaving the house, heading straight for them."

To understand this sort of dream, it is important to ask the question, "Who is Godzilla?" and then sit with it for a few days or weeks and let the answers come. This is an exciting dream, because Godzilla is such a powerful, evil, nasty force. There is nothing redeeming about Godzilla. Our movie-going experience identifies King Kong as big and strong, but he also showed some tenderness, and was really mean only when provoked. Godzilla, on the other hand, is mean and terrorizing, and is capable of interrupting anyone's life. It is difficult to not pay attention to Godzilla, because, when he enters your house, you automatically react in fear and panic. Godzilla demands that you be afraid and run for your life. This is exactly what happens in the dream. He has come in and interrupted whatever peace and tranquility there may have been in the house. The problem with Godzilla is that you cannot deal with him in the present tense; his force is too powerful, and your only choice is to escape. Even dealing with Godzilla in the future doesn't help, because you don't want to have to deal with him after the fact, after he has already rampaged. The best time to deal with Godzilla is before he comes, and that is exactly why he comes in the dream "ahead of time," as a type of warning.

From a spiritual perspective, instead of saying that Godzilla is really evil and harmful, we can say that he represents an absence of anything positive. The lack of anything positive is the environment that gives birth to Godzilla. He feeds on negativity, where there is a lot of criticism, pessimism, depression, fear, hatred, envy, and other negative states. Godzilla comes in the dream before anything like him has really appeared. If we pay attention to this dream, it enables us to do something about it. We can create an environment that will allow for peace and development in positive ways. We are fortunate that Godzilla came in the dream and not in real life, because, metaphorically speaking, when he comes in real life, he is going to cause a lot of destruction before we can stop him.

Godzilla is a dream that really helps us make a complete break from the past. You may be reading this book and thinking, "Isn't it nice to read a book about dreams and learn a few things about this phenomenon." Then you can put the book down and go back to your everyday life and keep doing the same things you have always done in the same way. Instead of listening for the profound messages in the dreams and believing that they can be transformational you think they are nice and continue living the same life. While the spiritual dimension is giving you Godzilla so that you will wake up, your material self is giving you "nice" so that you can be comfortable doing nothing about the conditions of the world. You go to sleep at night and your spirit is taking you to an important film about you and your importance in the world, but when you wake up you do whatever it takes to forget the message and go back to your "nice" life trying to keep things just how they are so that nothing negative will happen. But what you don't realize is that the dream world comes from the spiritual dimension and the spirit won't let you sleep to your potential. It insists that you wake up and change yourself so that you can change the world. Godzilla is a huge wake up call.

You don't have to pay attention to Godzilla. You can stuff him in the back of your mind and continue the nice life as if nothing needed to be changed and you don't have a part of it, but then one day Godzilla leaves the dream world and appears in the real world. You had the chance to deal with him in the world of meditation and reflection, but you continued to be "nice", and, in your niceness, he left the non-material and started wreaking havoc in the real world. Godzilla is a perfect example of how nothing that comes to you that is negative in the real world should come as a surprise. We get warnings and messages all the time in our dreams, but they are often and usually ignored because of our own personal culture of niceness. Dreams give you a chance to deal with him beforehand and this is their amazing power.

The solution to Godzilla is surprising. To defeat his appearance in the present or in the future, you have to create a culture of positive action. The surprising element is that it isn't the quantity of any particular act that matters. The introduction of seemingly small and insignificant acts that are easily multiplied can prevent Godzillas from appearing. For example, offering everyone you meet a smile and a friendly greeting; offering your seat to an elderly person on the bus; acknowledging an act of kindness; holding your tongue when someone makes a mistake; finding and praising the good rather than criticizing something negative. It is always amazing to me how, when a group is criticizing someone or something, the introduction of a positive comment quiets the Godzilla-like environment. It can't be overemphasized how important timing is here. Taking positive action in advance always works better than attempting to correct negative actions. Attempting to correct mistakes often requires the killing of Godzilla with force, and that doesn't guarantee his absence will be sustained. In fact, you can get so pre-occupied with the killing machine that you may not have the skills and qualities necessary to do the positive things. The primary force you have is the will to take action. To have a positive environment, it is much better to have both positive action and positive will than to just have a huge will to fight a destructive force. The idea is to implement positive action before Godzilla is given the opportunity to appear.

Look back in history to World War II. The culture of the German people at that time was not based upon a lot of positive feedback and encouragement, it was primarily negative. It took a huge force outside of Germany to destroy a Godzilla (Hitler), but it hasn't prevented other Godzillas from appearing, because only Godzilla himself was killed, not the culture of negativity that created him. If you talk to German people raised after the war, they will tell you that they were raised with the consciousness to be more questioning of authority, and you will find that they are very capable of engaging in good questioning practices. But a Godzilla was not able to rise up in the German state because of lack of questioning, he rose up because of the lack of positive action in the culture. The problem is that we didn't have a culture that was really positive in nature before the war; this created conditions for war that still exist today, all over the world. This is why the dreamer is facing Godzilla and movie-makers are still making movies about him. It means that a culture of positive action and encouragement does not exist. A solution is to go back into the past to understand what conditions created Godzilla and to attempt to change them before he reappears. Obviously, you cannot go back to the depression of the 1930s to change what happened in real life, but you can change the perceptions about what was happening.

The creation of a culture of positive action can lead to a civilization that is both prosperous and just. We work to change perceptions so that conditions that existed in the past are not sustained today. The first necessary perception is for human beings to believe that they are, by nature, positive spiritual beings who possess boundless positive creative energy. Their energy is capable of anything and everything, and each individual is important and can make a huge difference. Obviously, a contrary belief existed during the depression, because Godzilla preyed on the habit of blaming others. He seized quickly on people's weaknesses, because they didn't think that they mattered, and they believed that something outside of themselves was responsible for what was happening to them. Also, they could be fooled quickly, because they didn't believe in their true selves. They believed that things outside of themselves controlled the future, not their own actions. So someone began to tell them that they were better than others, and, because of this, many people thought that they could do whatever they wanted to others, and they did.

If they had understood that they were really amazing people, along with everyone else in the world, and that each one was capable of doing amazing things, and that great things could happen beyond our wildest imagination if we all worked together, Godzilla would never have appeared. But he did, and he is still appearing in the dream world. This means that many people still don't understand that they are positive spiritual beings who have an infinitude of positive energy, and that they are capable of doing positive things. The moment that this understanding enters the collective consciousness of humanity, peace and prosperity are truly possible.

The dreamer, along with the rest of us, has the responsibility for encouraging people to see themselves as powerful, positive beings. She could start by taking positive actions to awaken that consciousness in people. The next dream explains how to take the first steps. It shows that, despite the damage of the past, we are still capable of making our world into an incredible place. In the spiritual domain, one doesn't pass from one grade to the next based on chronological age. You stay where you are until you have learned what you need to learn.

Quotation

"Dost thou reckon thyself only a puny form
When within thee the universe is folded?"
—Bahá'u'lláh, The Seven Valleys and the Four Valleys

Meditation questions

1. Has the culture around you taught you that you are not important and that your actions do not matter? How has it taught you that?
2. Has the culture taught you that you are superior to others, that they are really blameworthy, and that they are causing you difficulties? How have you been taught that?
3. What is preventing you from believing that you are a truly powerful, spiritual human being capable of creating infinite good?
4. Who in your life has given you the most encouragement to be your true self? How does that person do it?

Summary of symbols used

Godzilla—total evil, using a superior negative force to do as you please
running away—not facing the fear
out of the house—separated from your true self
[women—relational nature
men—assertive nature]

Commonality of Symbols

A big evil drives us away from ourselves; women are more likely to escape the evil than men.

CHAPTER 12

UNABLE TO DO THE THING YOU WANT TO DO

Taking On the Hierarchy

"The next dream I was in a large house, sort of like a dormitory. I was in the bathroom with another girl and we were both about to get into two different showers on opposite ends of the bathroom. I had a big pile of dirty laundry with me that I wanted to put into the wash before I got into the shower, only someone's stuff was still in the washer and it was full of sticky soap and all grimy. I got really annoyed. I then got into the shower and suddenly got really scared because I realized that there was a crazy man just on the other side of the shower. I got out of the shower, got dressed and ran out into a large dining room full of people eating and talking. I sat down and my husband came up and I explained about the crazy man. He said he'd go find the man and talk to him and so off he went. A little bit later, he came back to me and said it was all worked out, but I knew that the man was still lurking waiting for me around the corner, wanting to kill me."

At the end of the preceding dream, there were a group of women and a group of men. The women got away, but the men were ready to be trampled by Godzilla. A logical question that arises from that situation is, "Why were the women able to escape, but not the men?" One explanation is that men have some physical capacities that enable them to do more things that require strength than women. However, given this ability, men are more susceptible to creating and living in a cultural of superior-inferior relationships. When they do this, their true selves may become repressed, and their behaviors may become more egotistical than spiritual. Women are less susceptible to this circumstance than men, because the culture of women is less hierarchical in the sense of superior-inferior relationships. Even though Godzilla (the big ego) was after them, the women were able to escape because their true selves were more in tact. When you live in a hierarchical world, sooner or later you are going to encounter Godzilla.

In this dream, a threatening crazy man is trying to sneak into her shower. This powerfully represents men's dominance threatening to rape her of her purity. In a world where competition and superiority matter, a hierarchy attempts to dominate through deception, stealing, and threatening. When women attempt to behave purely, they become vulnerable to being dominated by the world of the hierarchy. A person who participates in the world of men's hierarchies risks becoming a thief or a liar. In order to compete successfully for positions of authority, you have to think of yourself as superior to others and, when you do this, you lose your true self. Competitive hierarchies guarantee that a society will lose its spiritual harmony, its collective true self. Peace is impossible in superior-inferior relationships. A peaceful civilization is one where relationships are based upon equality, where supervisors are more likely to see themselves as lower than others rather than higher than others, because they look upon their work as serving the needs of others. When women try to act with purity of motive in competitive societies, they often are faced with a culture of thieves. The more hierarchical structures there are, the more thieves they need to watch out for. This is because of the disparities that exist in superior-inferior relationships. The dream also indicates that there is a very deceptive quality to the thief. When the husband goes out to deal with the thief, he believes that everything is going to be fine after talking to him, but she knows that it isn't.

Women's cultures usually have some "natural antibodies" against the hierarchical system of thieves. This is probably related to the fact that giving birth and raising children is done best in cooperation with others, rather than in isolation. In the next dream, you will see that women are much better prepared for a society of peace than men.

A solution to the problems presented in this dream is to analyze everything in the culture that creates a hierarchical world of gross inequalities, and then attempt to do exactly the opposite. For instance, if you are a supervisor charged with responsibilities over a set of employees, instead of making decisions by yourself, make them with as much input from your other staff members as possible. Instead of trying to find out where they are doing things incorrectly, find out what they are doing right; emphasize their strengths, and, instead of compiling a list of the problems, ask them to identify their challenges. Wherever you have individual responsibility over others, create a group and work together. Hierarchies are structures based upon the idea that one individual can control the whole show. In situations where one individual is controlling things, the very act of making a group automatically starts breaking up the hierarchy.

This dream's structure is interesting because in the end of the dream her husband thinks everything is taken care of, but she still feels that the intruder is lurking. This is an example where you must, when working with a negative dream, start your process at the end of the dream, rather than at the beginning. If she starts at the beginning, then she would think that the problem is with her impurity because she is unable to clean herself or her laundry (roles), but if however she begins in the end, she will recognize as we must that she has to deal with the way the culture of hierarchy robs people of their pure dreams. What makes hierarchies fall apart and be replaced with more cooperative structures is when everyone knows that there is thief governing things. When we find out that the leaders are thieves and it becomes well known, that is when they lose their power and their control falls apart. So the first step for her in the dream is to let everyone know that the thief is still present. The leaders of hierarchies don't mind lying and cheating and stealing because that is how they get what they want, but when everyone knows that they can't be trusted, then they start to lose their power. Their power exists in deception and hiding; not in being seen. When you bring down a hierarchy, then you can start on the true dreams with purity because it is our nature to work in groups cooperatively like teams. Cooperation and teamwork make the power of each individual multiply and be much greater than when they function alone.

This dream teaches that our true nature is cooperative, but that we must resist the pressure of the culture that has corrupted that nature by creating systems of superiority-inferiority. Unfortunately we are still living in time where hierarchies are the rule and cooperation is the exception. We can overcome it by naming the ego of domination and thievery and then forming powerful groups that exist on the principle of mutuality.

"God loves who work in groups."

Meditation questions

1. How does the hierarchical world convince you that you are really wrong and off track when you are going for what you really want to do?
2. Make a list of the worse kinds of abuses you face in a system based upon authoritarian hierarchy.
3. Analyze behaviors done by leaders in an authoritarian hierarchy that take you away from being more effective, and then write contrasting behaviors that you would consider empowering.
4. Experiment by attempting behaviors that contrast with hierarchical things. Start at a place of low risk, and then gradually see if you can do the same thing in all parts of your life. Form a group.

Summary of symbols used

laundry—desire to clean up roles

shower—purifying of self

crazy man—men's dominating culture infringing on the true motives of women

trying to talk a crazy man into sense—attempting to help men understand the dangers of an authoritarian culture

Commonality of symbols

Impurity facing purity. When women try to do things more consistent with who they are, they run up against the negative aspects of men's culture.

CHAPTER 13

WOMEN'S DECEPTION

Turning Away from Materialism

"The next dream I was in a large department store and was waiting in line to buy something with my husband. He started flirting with another girl in line, so much that he didn't even notice when I got upset and left. I walked out of the store and decided to walk home, which was going to take me an hour and a half. I knew that he would eventually try to call me and find out where I was when he realized I was gone, so I turned off my cell phone."

Many of the difficulties women face with the power structure of society come from their need to have money and to buy things. When they enter the department store and see things that they want to have, they realize that the only way to get it is with money. The only way to get money is to participate in the system of the hierarchy because it promises money. Without money, you have nothing. In the previous dream, she was having problems doing the purifying work that her heart would have her do, because the thief was skulking around the door trying to take her purity away. In this dream, temptation is knocking on her husband's door, because the system still tempts him. He was already fooled by the thief; now the thief has become a woman, luring him out of his true self and into the world of deception so that someone else can control him.

The dreamer is really upset at the husband, because, while she is attempting to act as her true self in pure ways, she is not able to get what she wants. In the world of spirituality and growth, there is no flirting with the other side. The other side is the world of the ego. Its purpose in temptation is to take you away from your true self long enough that it can control you. She already understands the temptation, but she doesn't quite understand how to turn to her true self and get things happening in a positive way. She does the right thing in cutting off communication with her husband, because as long as he is flirting with the world of the ego, they are not able to work together to create positive things.

This is a difficult position for the dreamer to be in, because in the world of the hierarchy it is tempting to give in a little and take on a few impurities so that you can get a few extra material things in life. However, for her true self there can be no concession, so she does the right thing by leaving. The only problem with leaving is that it often generates feelings of loneliness and isolation. To go against the way things are and to be true to yourself is something that you always must do for yourself first. People will join you later, but in the beginning it is the ultimate leap of faith. She turns off the cell phone and starts the long walk home. But she can turn the whole situation around by turning on her "inner" cell phone and communicating with her true self. Her true self will teach her how to fly and move rapidly from one place to another. Her true self will get her whatever she needs and she will inspire others. When you are living out of your true self, others always join you, but, if you give into your ego, you eventually lose all of your relationships. The first and most important relationship is with your own true self, because it is connected to the larger spiritual world and teaches you how to make lasting connections.

Her primary emotion in the dream is anger. Being angry with others almost always indicates that you are also angry about something in your own self. It is a mirror-like emotion and, except in cases of abuse or gross injustice, you always have to take a look at what you are really attached to materially. You then have to let go of it, go for the non-material positive energy, and your life will start to fly. Her husband is a mirror of her own self. Both of them have gone to the department store and are waiting in line to get their "deserved" share of the material benefits of the world. Fortunately, she turns away from it and starts the long journey toward her true bliss. Turning off the cell phone and resorting to walking is such a positive action that there is no way you can ever overestimate it and, because of it, lots of people's lives will be better. She has turned away from the material world and started the journey toward her true self, her bliss. By doing so, she will be creating the culture that allows others to do the same. The only difficulty is that she is angry. When you show your anger to people in the material world, they often move further away from you. If she wants to include others, she first must talk with her self to find out what to do with her life. Then her heavy, trudging footsteps and weariness will change into soaring and flying. The spiritual world will open up to her and her life will start to live out its purpose.

It is not easy; it is an extreme act of will to turn off the cell phone and live truly.

Spiritual work on major issues always follows of sequence of four steps and it is very helpful to know when you analyze dreams where you are in the four-step process. The first step is to face a major fear as in facing Godzilla. You need to face fear and transform it so that you can begin on the journey and have enthusiasm and courage about the future. The second step involves getting rid of thieves and cheats that try to get you take short cuts from the path. This keeps you headed in the right direction after you have taken the initial steps. In this dream she goes for the third step which is to turn your heart away from materialism so that it can see true beauty and fall in love with what it is doing. Fortunately for her it is just a flirtation rather than an all out affair with the other side. In the next dream she faces the final step which is commitment and determination.

Questions for meditation

1. What is the biggest lure for me in the material world that takes me away from doing the things I truly want to do?
2. Make a list of activities that you can do that are in line with your true goals and then make plans to do them.
3. Commit 15 minutes each day to scheduling and doing activities that are truly in line with your true goals.
4. Using some magazines, make a visual representation of the things you want to be doing and put it in a place where you will see it each day, such as in your journal.

Summary of symbols used

department store—a place to get the things that you need in order to do what you need to
flirting—temptation to go away from true self toward the ego
cell phone—a means of communicating
turning off cell phone—refusing to communicate

Commonality of Symbols

The symbols teach the person the necessity to first do inner communication through meditation, and then to beginning acting. Then the resources will be made available.

CHAPTER 14

WHO'S KNOCKING AT MY DOOR

Committed to the End

"The last dream I had, I was staying in a motel room with my husband. An old friend came up and was knocking on our door, but it took us a long time to hear and answer it. By the time we got there, he was already walking away. I called his name over and over again until finally I screamed his name really loudly and he heard me, turned around and came back to talk to us. He asked us if he could borrow $700 to buy a vacuum cleaner. I said sure, but that we'd have to go to a bank. We decided to meet at a store. By the time I got there, I found my husband, but could not find the old friend anywhere. I got frustrated with my husband because he had lost the old friend and was distracted with something else. We bumped into some friends at the store and they offered to drive us around the town to try to find him. We started driving around, stopping in different places, but couldn't find him. Finally we reached an area where the road ended and foot path began. We all got out of the car and walked and walked and walked until we reached a school. Inside the school we found another old friend who was in a bad mood because she was waiting for everyone else to show up for a dance workshop practice and they were all late."

This dream starts at a motel. A motel means that you are outside of your own city on the highway symbolizing that she is already on her journey of actualizing her plans. The visitor is a person who consistently shows partial commitment, tentativeness.

He first knocks, but walks away, then asks but doesn't show up at the place where they agreed to meet, and as a result they never find him, but go to the end of the road with nothing and find a person who is angry at others for being late.

The purpose of the dream is to show the nature of tentativeness. It shows how necessary firmness of commitment is and that just asking and making an agreement isn't enough. In order to be successful with any endeavor there needs to be a commitment to action that is strong both from yourself and from others. Her commitment is strong because she yells for the other person to come back and then sets up a meeting time and drives all over the town to find him. Her problem is that she doesn't recognize how weak the commitment of the other person is. So she just gets mad and ends up with nothing and finds people who are in the same situation as her.

For a project to work, especially the type of projects the dreamer wants to do in conjunction with others, she needs to find others who will make a similar commitment. Jesus says in the Bible that he doesn't like those who are lukewarm and so it is with the person knocking on the door. He has nothing to give and just wants a vacuum cleaner to suck the life out of others so that he can have the advantage. At this stage she needs to let him go and find others who are committed, join together and do great work.

The woman at the end of the road is one such person and the clue that they are both suited for each other is that she is also angry which means that she is committed but can't exact a commitment from others. The major connection to this dream is the dream that began with Chapter 11 with Godzilla. When you are dealing with a major issue in your life, it often begins with a big fear such as the fear of Godzilla and then ends in the fourth dream with a call to commitment. The beginning is a fear that keeps you from entering the action and the end is the energy that keeps you from being able to finish.

The four steps are usually a combination of courage and enthusiasm, purity and independence of thinking, love for what you are doing and communication with self and others, and finally commitment to finish what you start with confidence. Every life issue takes you through these stages and sometimes they take years to overcome depending on the issue. At different stages a different energy will appear which needs to be actualized in order for your life to work at that moment. The spiritual world always knows the correct path and will always send the information to you. It is faithful to the end. It seems to me that the spiritual world prefers to send information beforehand to you so that you will know what to do and how to face your life truly, but if you don't pay attention to the dreams or other types of spiritual communication you will get all that you need to wake up and become aware in your daily life. You can not escape what the soul wants from you, and it will be persistent much more so than you can ever imagine. Your life is meant to follow a really good path so that you can do great things and if you can deal with the problems before they happen in real life, they will be less severe and take less of toll on yourself.

She should therefore, be really grateful, as I am for Godzilla appearing as well as the person without commitment. She has to face and deal with the world where Godzilla is possible, and so she needs to find others who want something different. Godzilla is a blessing because the end of the series of dreams is in the beginning dream. You can say that the end of all things is in the beginning. Every dream tells you the end in the beginning. The end is the thing you are going for, the goal, the purpose, the vision. It comes in the beginning and sometimes it appears violently to let you know that it isn't going to be easy. Who wants to face Godzilla? Nobody! But you can face Godzilla if you make a mirror of him from his negative image into the huge positives that exist spiritually. If you don't have a big potential, Godzilla never appears because it means that you are not capable of overcoming big challenges.

Godzilla comes to awaken the immensity of who we really are and then when we truly believe it and act on it, Godzilla disappears because he is no longer necessary and knows his fate is sealed before he appears.

What this dream is saying at the end is that when you get to the end of the road and all you have is anger with nothing concrete, you need to turn around 180 degrees and go to the beginning. Because you will find what you want, your end in the beginning, by looking at the opposite of Godzilla. She needs to remind herself of her purpose and when she does so, the road will be a place of wonder and awe and it will take her to yet undreamt of realities.

We say in English that we are at the end of our rope. This means that we have reached the end of everything we know how to do and still haven't gotten the results. So the dreamer can start getting great results by going back to the beginning and remembering the vision which is the positive opposite of Godzilla. Most likely her end has a lot to do with beauty, creativity, and creating new structures because Godzilla is the opposite of all this. In a hierarchical world of power creativity is the most threatening of all virtues because it doesn't respect top-downness. This dream shows that she starts on her path, on our path of creativity by having a vision of something new and then finding others who are committed to the same things.

When you have enough force and movement, then you can transform the ones who were tentative into firm adherents, but not at the beginning. They only suck the energy of the group or the vision. The four dreams give her a basis of how to face the issue of living in the world, the culture the way it is with mainly hierarchical, non egalitarian structures. She is given a balance of virtues so that she can face the world with confidence. In the dreams that follow she will be shown how to make her skills really effective so that they can achieve their purpose.

Questions for Meditation

1. When am I most likely to be tentative in my life?
2. Who is it in my life that sucks out energy and is uncommitted and how does he make his way into my life? Am I contributing to his staying?
3. What is the larger vision that keeps me motivated and into life fully committed?
4. Write down a list of things that you are angry about and then think about what you are angry at yourself about and then start facing the problem inside yourself.

Summary of symbols used

motel—temporary resting spot for the self along the journey of life
old friend who walks away—lack of commitment
knocking on the door—uncommitted trying to interfere with commitment
vacuum cleaner—sucking life out of things
bank—place to get into debt
driving around not finding the old friend—chasing uncommitted gets you nowhere
road ended—foot path began—walked and walked—consequence of not having a firm commitment; things just go on and on with no results
angry and frustrated—emotions related to not accomplishing the goals

Commonality of symbols

The symbols are showing that on the journey of life commitment is everything if you want to finish what you have started. You go into debt, get the life sucked out, and just go on and on with nothing unless you have commitment.

CHAPTER 15

UNIFYING ALL THE PAST

Making Peace By Following the Generation to Come

". . . I was at a Chinese cultural event/birthday party. The room was filled with friends of mine from the past and we were all eating, talking and hanging out. I was talking with one of my best friends from elementary school, who had married an Asian boy from my high school. Suddenly she turned into one of my high school girl friends, and her husband started telling me about how he started on some herbal supplements a year ago that drastically improved his love life. Then I was outside walking with another high school friend. We were walking to get ice cream. Suddenly I realized that this was not normal, because she had been incarcerated. I asked her how she was able to leave the jail to be here for the party. She just shrugged her shoulders. We continued walking."

This dream shows the results of having done the work in the previous dreams and how everything becomes a continuous line from the issues she has worked through in the past up the present. This is a "persuasive" dream that is trying to give her confidence to continue on the path which she has chosen. It reminds her of difficulties that have all been turned into victories and strengths, because she has faced them all successfully. They are now positives, so she can continue forward and go for it.

A Chinese event means that she is in the culture that is furthest away from her own and having a great time. This is an amazing symbol, because it means that she has achieved the ability to be a great peace maker. She is in a different culture, having a relaxing time and experiencing the complete integration of the east and west. This integration also extends into how she can get healthy in a physical way, because she has already experienced spiritual union. Finally, she gets to the most incredible part of the dream. She is walking freely with a person who in real life is in prison. This is a result of walking your own spiritual path. It gives you freedom wherever you are and makes the impossible possible. The person in prison doesn't know how she was able to walk freely because she doesn't know that it is the dreamer who gave her the power to walk freely. In this dream, the dreamer is totally unaware of her gifts and how much she helps establish unity for others. She has brought unity to people because she does everything in a natural, relaxed process. As long as she stays relaxed and enjoys it, miracles will happen.

I am in complete awe of the dreamer in this dream. She is a person I would readily follow, even though I am her father. I wish I could take credit for the gifts she has and the way she brings unity and freedom to people, but I can only say that I am fortunate to be associated with her in a special way. I have tried to play my part, but I recognize that her energy and purpose are much greater than mine and come from some other domain. We know that life is progressive and civilization is advancing, but when you see your own offspring advancing way beyond your own self, you can only sit back and be in awe of the bounties that the Creator bestows upon all beings. She is a bringer of unity and it shows in this dream. She liberates others.

In this dream, the past and the future and the present come together to be a timeless energy that she will use forever, and from which we all can learn. Have a party with people that are the most different culturally from you and it will bring healing and complete freedom to the world. This message is simple and profound. We can follow her example in the dream and bring peace to the world.

Meditation Questions

1. Make a list of people who are very different than yourself and think about ways to include them in your life. For instance, if you are a supervisor, work on your relationship with the cleaning people. If you are white, have a relationship with a black person.
2. Make a timeline chart of your life and write the major events that have shaped your strong qualities
3. Describe the negative emotion that most keeps you back from other people, especially people who are different from you.
4. Think about the thing inside of you that most makes you who you are in a very positive way. What are your strongest positive qualities and how do they make the world a better place for people to live in?

Summary of symbols used

Chinese cultural event—shows the dreamer integrating something very different from herself to make it a part of her.

Relationship of two different cultures—part of a three part process::—first association, then integration and, finally, the fruits of the dream.

herbal remedies—the positive results of harmonizing opposites, differences

freeing from jail—inner freedom that comes from integration of extremes

Commonality of symbols

The symbols are used to show us that when you integrate opposites or extremes or differences, you get really positive results.

CHAPTER 16

THE BRIDE IS THE GROOM
AND THE GROOM IS THE BRIDE

Understanding through Contrast

"I had a dream this morning that I was getting ready for a wedding. We rushed there and were a little bit late. Just as I sat down in the front row, the ceremony began. Sitting right in front of me were the bride and groom, only the bride was wearing a tux and the groom was wearing a wedding gown (and everyone was saying how beautiful it was). In the dream, I knew the guy who was getting married, but I can't remember who it is now, (someone from high school, I think). I didn't know the bride.

When the ceremony was over, I was asked to paint the floor black so that the guests could write things on it. I had to mix my own paints and come up with my own paintbrush. I used a long piece of paper that I rolled up; I put paint on it, then unrolled it across the floor. It seemed to work pretty well, but my paint wasn't very dark, so the floor didn't get very black.

After I finished with that, I went outside for a walk and bumped into the groom. We were looking for flowers to bring back into the house when he confessed to me that he was actually in love with me all this time. Just then the bride walked up and, seeing us, got jealous and stomped off."

This is a very interesting dream about the dreamer as an artist. Her purpose in life is a creative one, as was mentioned in a previous dream, and the way she can portray things begins to be unfolded in this dream. In the spiritual world, there is a type of oneness and harmony that is not understood by human minds. In fact, we are not capable of understanding the kind of oneness that exists in the spiritual dimension; our best approximation is in the world of the metaphor. One way to compare the oneness of the Creator is to think of energy like the sun. When you look at the sun, you only see a bright light. This light has the quality of brightness, but you don't see differentiated colors. The power of the light is so strong to our eyes that if we look directly into it for more than an instant, it begins to hurt our eyes and eventually damages them. Only when the individual rays emanating from the sun reach the earth do we begin to differentiate the limitless colors, shapes, and other perceptual dimensions. A leaf, for instance, absorbs all the rays from the sun except the color green, which it reflects. And a berry on a plant may absorb all the sun's rays except the red. A bird may see lots of green leaves that all look the same, but then it will see the contrasting red of the berry. The berry with the quality of sweetness gives him nourishment and sustains his life so that he can continue flying and living. Without the contrast of colors, he would just see one single bright light and it would be impossible for him to survive. The differentiation of the way things absorb the rays of the sun gives them their qualities. Without contrast, there is no separation of qualities.

Our minds need contrast and differentiation so that we can achieve understanding. Without differentiation, there is no understanding in the mind. In the dream, we are presented with a wedding, which is a symbol of union, of integration. You have two distinct entities coming together to form one union. In the spiritual world, there is never a problem with union, because qualities that emanate from the same spiritual source automatically unite. When you have developed one quality and then work on another one, they will work together in a harmonious way. As they are developing, you don't have to work on their union. As we work to develop a quality, the first thing that we need to do is to understand its qualities. Let's say that you would like to be more enthusiastic.

First, you need to know what the quality is and how it acts in the world. You don't have to worry about whether it will combine with perseverance or honesty; that will be automatic.

The way you get to know the differentiated nature of a quality is by understanding its negative opposites. The opposite of enthusiasm is some form of depressive energy. Enthusiasm excites you to go forward, whereas its opposite depresses you to slow you down. When you don't have a lot of enthusiasm, you have something that is depressing you, slowing you down, and it will show up in the dream.

The problem in the dream is that the bride is the groom and the groom is the bride. This means that they are both trying to be the same. This is a type of conformity in which they are trying to blend into the culture, rather than letting their good qualities stick out in great contrast. The idea of a marriage is to bring your best qualities to it, for, when you do so, the marriage works. The positives automatically unite. When you try to be like the other person, or like everyone else, then you get monotony, which becomes boring, and then you don't have the energy to make it happen.

For the dreamer, the dream does not represent a lot of negative feeling; the dream is there to teach her a lesson about her artwork, about her life. She is already creative and resourceful; she is making her own materials. She needs to learn just how important contrast really is; it is the most important lesson in this dream. What could make the wedding work is contrast, but, instead, there is too much trying to blend in. If you work with pigments, blending turns into blah, whereas contrast gives you understanding and energy. This is what is needed. The dream is trying to teach the artist to paint with contrast, to bring all of her true self into the work, to use the darkest dark to bring out the lightest light.

When you have gone through a depression, a personal darkness, and come out the other end, you not only have enthusiasm and energy for life, but you also have understanding about the nature of the energies. This makes you much more competent than relying merely on enthusiasm. At the end of this dream, the bride becomes jealous because the groom really loves the artist. He probably was too busy trying to blend in to notice how much he loved the person who was being her true self. The bride becomes jealous, the emotion of protection, because she thinks that she has to blend in; she also is fearful of not being able to be her true self.

The metaphors in this dream are exquisite. It seems to me that it is trying to make the dreamer lead a life of true contrast to others. It also is showing her how to paint in a contrasting style, which will bring out everything positive in the end. In the first step of a union between people or groups, contrast is important because it gives understanding. Once you have understanding, you can move to the next domain. This is where the bride truly is the groom and the groom is in the bride. They have both learned important lessons from each other in the relational work. They have learned each other's value and have released the other quality within themselves; oneness really does exist, and it matters not who is who. To try to do it without the understanding is the mistake.

As an artist, the dreamer must first paint with contrast, using a dark darkness so that the light will become very apparent. When the light appears, we will know why we needed the darkness. The darkness will then become the source of illumination, so that the dark is light and the light is dark.

A soldier can not know courage unless he has been in a battle where he has to face intense fear. Out of the fear comes the courage. It is only with the experience of the fear that you can learn how to become more courageous. Without the fear, your ability to grow is minimal. Contrast is our great teacher; without it, we know nothing about life and we develop nothing. There just seems to be an abundance of things that our conscious minds won't accept without the real life experience to teach us something. When I did bungy jumping with my daughters, I had so much fear running through my body that it was like a river of negative energy passing through every part. My eyes must have been telling my brain that I was going to die for sure if I jumped, because the height would mean death. I t could not accept that the bungy chord would protect me. The only way I could jump was to keep telling myself that no one was dying. The experience taught my brain that it was safe to jump and that I could actually enjoy myself. Without the experience of facing the fear and overcoming it, I had no way of knowing this, even watching other people only mildly helped.

There seems to be a point in between the energy of the fear and the enthusiastic rush of flying, in which you just have to say something like, "What the hell! Let's go for it!" The fear lets go and the spirit takes over and then you fly. Most of the decisions about your future and taking new steps are like this. Everything leading up to making the decision and going for it is a way to abate the fear inside. Once you make the decision and go for it, the spirit can begin to release and provide inspiration. Facing the future is always a courageous act. When you are no longer fearful of the future, it means that the fear has turned itself into courage and enthusiasm, just as the darkness becomes the means for showing the light in the paintings.

Meditation Questions

1. What is it that you are blending into in the culture that is taking you to a place where you don't really want to be?
2. What is the worst kind of darkness that you are facing in your life now and what is its positive lightness?
3. When does jealousy take over your life?
4. What is the fear that holds your future back?

Summary of symbols used

wedding—integration of two energies, two parts
bride and groom wearing each other's clothes—necessity to take away labels and words and classifying when you are in the realm of integration; acceptance of the other being the same as you.

painting the floor black—need for contrast
looking for flowers—pursuit of beauty
wife being jealous—protecting oneself from integration

Commonality of symbols

The symbols show that when you integrate two parts you acquire one energy that can take on either role. First you need to have the two parts contrasted, so that they can be understood and then integrated.

CHAPTER 17

FLYING ON LAND AND WATER

Admiring Difficult Issues

"Dad, I had this dream the other day: I was in the Northwest Territories. It was night time, or so I thought; it was all dark out and we were being driven somewhere in a motor boat. We were going really fast and kind of flying over the water and pieces of land. The water was dark except for glimmerings of aqua green like the Caribbean. Then we got to a house where there was a bunch of people. I didn't really like what was going on, so I went outside. I looked at the sky and the sun was totally eclipsed by the full moon, except for a ring of fire around it. It was beautiful. And I kept pointing it out to other people around."

Many dreams are truly astonishing. The dreamer goes off into the dream world and, when she wakes up, she discovers that she has been to the land of astonishment. Astonishment is an emotion that brings us extremely close to the spiritual world, so close that it seems we are traveling in it. When you rip away the veils of the physical world and soar in the astonishment of the spiritual world, the rules extend beyond what was the major law of the material world, gravity, and give way to wonder and awe, which allow you speed across the world of unknowns.

This dream is in the Northwest Territories of Canada, the northernmost part of the country. Usually the north is the place of the mind. The mind is the place of illumination, because it is through the prism of the mind that light is shed on things so that we can come to an understanding about them and then begin to use them and transform them into positive realities. In this dream, however, she is going to a place where the mind has been eclipsed and, except for a few glimmerings, the people have remained in darkness. What she needs to know is that, in the world of darkness and the eclipsed selves of others, she can swiftly move across the water like a boat. In other words, even though the darkness exists and the lights from others are not visible, she has no problems moving and functioning at her best even to the point of feeling awe. This is the ability to be able to see the light in the darkness, to see peace in war, or to see love in hatred. It isn't that the darkness is positive in itself, but you understand that the contrasting reality of darkness is light. When you can see a problem and experience amazement, it means that you don't regard problems as permanent. You understand them to be circumstances that can transform from a negative into a positive.

A problem with contemporary psychology is its lack of a spiritual foundation; it tends to see peoples' problems as fixed objects, as if they were material things. Spiritual psychology is based on the foundation that everything is in a state of constant motion and that a problem is already in motion as you are describing it. In cultures with a more spiritual foundation, such as aboriginal cultures, their language tends to be more verbally oriented, as if everything is alive and moving. Cultures that have a basis in material things tend to be more noun-oriented, as if things have a permanently changeless nature. For instance, it is very difficult to deal with a person who is experiencing a lot of negative energy if you portray him a depressed person. By doing so, you have turned his behaviors (verb) into his identity (noun). It would be more useful to talk about how he is depressing himself, how he slows himself way down. Material healing may focus on the condition as if it were permanent, convincing the person that they will probably have to take medications for the rest of their lives. Such treatment persuades people that depression is part of who they are. Spiritual healing believes that problems are temporary. It may help a person to be assisted by material means, but treating and healing the spiritual condition can help the person to resolve the problem and experience recovery.

As in the dream, a therapist is awed and impressed by peoples' darkness and eclipsed states, rather than overwhelmed or defeated by them. They may look at a problem and say, "Wow! That's a big one!" They work systematically to uncover the structure of the difficulty and then work to change it into a positive asset by doing its opposite. They may do this for themselves as well as helping others. These are the people who march into hell and say, "Aren't there are a lot of interesting problems here?" They may even get a charge out of irritating the devil just to see what his reaction would be. For them, the devil is not an immortal evil person who tries to do harm to everyone. Evil is a negative energy that people may transmit, but that energy also can be transformed into a positive force. In this dream we are taught the value of living a life of astonishment, whether it be in light or in darkness.

I have worked with many people who believe that things are fixed and permanent. This is hard, because if their problem really was permanent, it couldn't be changed. In fact, it already is changing; if a person doesn't deal with them, their problems always get worse. They can move forward or backward, but they are never stationary, because the internal push in human beings is for growth and change, not immutability.

This dream is telling us about peace. We can't achieve peace unless we are willing to understand the structure of war. To understand war, you need to be able to see it with a certain amount of awe. You can actually see how a solution will emerge by seeing how the conflict is being played out. In the Northwest Territories, there is a conflict between European culture and Aboriginal culture. A conflict like this can only be solved by each group seeing the best parts about the other culture, praising those parts sincerely, incorporating them into their own cultures, and then being really vigilant and determined to look at their own culture and systematically change the weaknesses into strengths. But it needs people like the dreamer, people who are in awe of the eclipse, who see the end in the beginning, who see peace emerging from war, and unity emerging from the separation.

When most people encounter a conflict, they consider it awful. But our dreamer arrives and says, "Wow, what an awesome eclipse!" She is motivated by the conflict, because in it she sees peace itself. She doesn't fight with it or use the strategy of blame. She stands in awe of it, which is the only way that you can approach solving it in the long run. In the middle of a conflict, most of us see only our own point of view and blame the other side for the problems. This has the effect of entrenching the problem. Even a superior use of force by one side only temporarily upsets the balance of power. Force and resistance in a conflict only makes things worse. The solution to a conflict is to submit to it, that is, to understand that it is there because it needs to be there. When it is solved, everyone benefits.

In Aboriginal cultures, the positive values include living harmoniously with everything, respecting the wisdom that has gone on before, and generously sharing everything that you have. In European cultures, the value is to leave the past behind and set out for new discovery, so that life can get better. With both cultures, the values benefit each other and they should be honored. It was because of the Europeans that the aboriginal cultures received a language in which they could all communicate. Many of the modern technologies that tie people together over great distances are a result of the discovery process. Likewise, the aboriginal people had a democratic form of government, even a type of federated system, long before the Europeans. These things can be appreciated and honored.

What can not be done is the habit of looking at the other side and pointing the finger of blame so that you don't have to deal with your own difficulties. We know by our nature that we are imperfect and this gives us the bounty of always being able to find places where we can improve. If we look at ourselves, find the places that need improving, and then actively reform them, we always will make progress, and then the world gets better. But if we do the opposite, then we become entrenched in a power conflict that only ends with things getting worse.

Meditation Questions

1. What is the most important conflict that I am now having in my life?
2. What is it that I need to learn through the conflict I am having? (If you get the learning the conflict will end.)
3. What is it that is preventing me from seeing the positive qualities in people who are different from me, or with whom I am feeling uncomfortable?
4. Where and when am I most likely to get into a state of awe?

Summary of symbols used

Northwest territories—place furthest north associated with mental strengths Speeding over water in the dark—the ability to work easily in relationships that have been darkened, or with people who are having great difficulties Eclipse—people who have abilities that have been covered up by difficulties or trauma House where people were with difficulties—recognition by feeling of people's negative aspects Awe—being amazed with life, even in the face of dealing with people with huge problems

Commonality of symbols

The symbols show that one can work easily with people who have experienced great trauma or people who are dealing with great difficulties, because a great huge light is always behind the darkness in people. When you believe in the light you can be in awe of an eclipse.

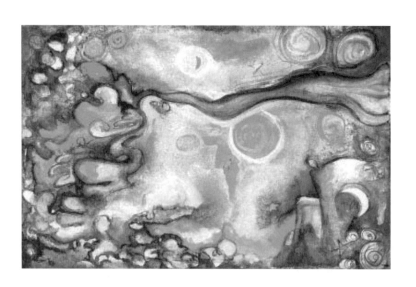

CHAPTER 18

THE INVISIBLE MAN

Becoming Detached from the World Around Us

(First Dream)

"I was in some sort of shopping mall near an escalator. In the mall there were a lot of people looking for me. All of them had weapons and had a very ominous presence. I was hiding and they couldn't see me. Then I had this feeling that I could be invisible, that is, I could just walk right by them and they would not be able to see me. So I did, and they didn't see me."

(Second Dream)

"I was in a prison camp and people were about to torture me. I decided that I could just walk out and I did. No one did anything; they couldn't touch me."

One of the wonderful things about dreams is that you often find yourself doing things that, in waking life, you are completely unable to do. For instance, you can walk through walls or fly or jump really far. The purpose of these dreams is to show you, through the appropriate metaphor, spiritual abilities that exist inside of yourself. When you learn the inner meaning and can release the energy from inside of yourself, you will be able to function in your life with a lot more competence. It isn't that after this dream I would be able to be invisible, but there is something about the energy that enables me to be more competent and guarded, as if I were invisible.

The end of both of these dreams is invisibility. That is, I am capable of walking away from the danger in both circumstances. Being invisible means to go "inside" yourself, into the invisible realm. In the dreams, the problems occur in the beginning. The end is positive, but the beginning is negative. This means that I already am capable of accessing my true self in the invisible realm, which is positive. In the beginning, my fears create a situation that do not allow the invisibility to flourish in real life. Invisibility works in my dream life, not in my waking life, because my fears are too intense to let it happen. In dream-work, the goal always is to make everything positive, to systematically work through the dreams so that each negative aspect is transformed into a contrasting, positive activity. When you do the transformation work, you end up with positive upon positive, thereby increasing your competency. When I work through the fears presented in the dream, it will not only allow the invisibility to fully function, it will also release the energy that has been repressing my fears. When I work through this, it is like a double bonus. It actually shows the double value of invisibility, both in positive situations and in negative ones.

These dreams present two of my fears that are closely related: the fear of being shot down and the fear of being tortured. I always find it easier to work on an issue that I can take responsibility for, so I try not to blame others for my fears, even when I have been in situations where people have behaved badly. As long as I characterize them as the culprits and myself as the victim, I am less capable and have little control over the situation. When I am both the culprit and the victim of my own inadequate inner workings and negative patterns, I know that I can do something about them. However, making such an assertion and actually doing something about it are two different things. Something is so universal, so easy, so temporarily satisfying about blaming others. People rarely escape its seductive attraction. When I do my own personal work, I usually start out being furious toward someone else. I blame them and pin lots of guilt on them. Then I slowly and laboriously work through the problem until I find that, whatever I have accused the other person of doing to me, I already am doing to myself. It is a major blow to the ego when you come to the realization that you are the guilty party and you are doing it to yourself. It also is a huge blessing, because the fears can be transformed into positive opposites, resulting in new abilities and new patterns of positive energy. The energies released from the negative aspects of the dreams are actually a blessing; they make the therapeutic work much easier.

Usually when you have fear, you are facing a situation that already has played itself out in your life, often repeatedly. This is a little different from anxiety, which is an emotion that makes an illusion out of a future negative possibility. Anxiety is related to an illusion, whereas fear is usually based on experience, sometimes the experiences of parents who pass the fear down through their negative responses to things. Even cultures pass down fears based upon negative sentiments about past events. In the two dreams presented here, the origin of the fears doesn't really matter. I have shot myself down and tortured myself repeatedly. Consequently, studying my dreams may reveal some new understanding, but it will always have the same result, the blocking of a fully functional ability to act with invisibility (spiritual qualities).

When I stop putting myself down and stop torturing myself, then invisibility will be more accessible. This is the goal of the dream. Unlike waking life, in the dream life the end of things comes at the beginning, because the spiritual world wants you to know your purpose, your goal, your objective, before you begin acting. The purpose of the dream is to get me to stop putting myself down and to stop torturing myself, so that invisibility can work. In order to stop doing the negative things, I need to do their positive opposites, which then will allow the really positive energy to flow.

When I meditate about these dreams, the intrigue first wraps itself up in the ability to be invisible. However, as my understanding increases, the real jewels are in the positive opposites of the negative emotional states. I know that I have the ability to be invisible even without understanding what it is. It is something that I already am competent in intuitively, but I am not yet adept at just letting it flow and work as it wants to. This is because I am forever putting myself down and torturing myself. Overcoming these dreadful patterns is the work. Putting yourself down and then torturing yourself to make sure that you stay down is universal; it exists in every culture. It is hard to imagine that we could ever have peace in the world unless we change these characteristics of humanity. People have patterns of behavior based upon the false belief that criticizing others and pointing out their faults will improve them. All around the world, people believe it, even though study after study verifies that the opposite is true. Many people believe that when you point out to someone what they are doing wrong, they know where to improve. However, the research indicates that when you criticize people and are negative toward them, they feel less motivated, tend to quit more easily, and have poorer relationships.

If I would do the opposite of putting myself down and torturing myself through criticism, blaming and guilt-mongering, I could be more motivated, stay with things longer, and have fantastic relationships. What are the opposites? The opposite of putting oneself down is lifting oneself up by acknowledging the positives and adhering to positive patterns rather than the negative ones. The opposite of torture is extreme gentleness, a quality that I have not practiced very well. Gentleness appeared in the giant teddy bear dream and it appears here again. Some people regard gentleness as a weakness. Gentleness allows weakness, but it isn't a weakness in itself. When you make room for weakness, it means that it is permissible to have flaws and faults. If gentleness is such a positive force, why do cultures shy away from its power?

We do not stay in the state of gentleness as a world culture, because, when we are faced with a fault or weakness, we experience discomfort. Instead of embracing the discomfort and learning from it, we run from it and then criticize and blame others. Gentleness allows us to embrace our imperfections, and then it helps us to transform them by making lots of room for them. When we lift ourselves up by finding the positives, and when we also have lots of room for imperfection, without having to be mean and nasty or turn away from it, then personal transformation is not only possible, it is an easy and smooth process. Imagine that you planned an event in which everything went well except for a few things. If you use these two strategies, not only are you likely to repeat success, but you also are likely to achieve a new level the next time you attempt it. In the evaluation process, you can spend the majority of the time reminding yourself of all of things that went well. When you do this, it fixes success in your memory; this makes it more automatic and habitual. This way, you can take the thing that is the biggest weakness and use it to develop new qualities within yourself. If you focus on the weakness, instead of the success, or if you focus too much energy on the weakness and not enough on the success, then you will be practicing the weakness. You will be diminishing or forgetting your success, which could result in your quitting the projects, becoming less motivated, and losing important relationships.

All new abilities first start in the world of ideas, the world of non-material reality, like the dream world, and then later they appear in action in the real world. A new building or piece of art doesn't create another new building. A new piece of art or new building emanates from new ideas, and new ideas are produced by their creators going into the realm of the invisible to do their creation. This is where you can find wonderful new ideas and energies. The best way to do it is by creating an extremely positive atmosphere and being really gentle with your weaknesses; you can work on them with the care and tenderness of a good nurse or a good doctor, whose presence allows healing to take place. When a baby is born into this world, mothers are instinctively gentle with their babies and almost always positive. They recognize the weaknesses of their children and give them lots of room and encouragement. This is how babies develop. However, somewhere in the process of development, of maturation, the whole world forgets how the baby developed. Imperfection is no longer given lots of space and embraced. Instead of being gentle and encouraging, we become harsh, and judgmental, and critical. Our fears take over and squeeze out the positive. We forget how easy success and transformation can be; we dwell on the negative things, and then quit things easily and have poor relationships. New ideas and new abilities come from this invisible realm, which is facilitated by remembering the positive and being gentle with our weaknesses as we work to transform them.

Summary of symbols used

People with weapons trying to kill the dreamer—feeling threatened
Being invisible—the positive quality of concealing faults
Being in prison and tortured—criticizing and punishing yourself;
     the prison of self
Walking away unnoticed—the ability to conceal negatives and
     emphasize positives

Commonality of symbols

The symbols are showing that when you stop criticizing and being fearful, when you conceal faults and work on them privately, you can be free to do what you want to do and to be your true self.

Meditation Questions

1. What is the worst thing people say about me? What is the positive opposite?
2. What else do people say about me that is critical? What are the positive opposites?
3. What other things do I criticize about myself? What are the positive opposites?
4. Write a paragraph about how your life would change if you lived out the opposites.

CHAPTER 19

LANDING ON ANOTHER PLANET

Moving from Loneliness to Togetherness

"I was somehow aware of being on another planet. The air was foggy and unclear and I was alone in the house with an uncomfortable feeling. It was a spooky feeling because of being alone and the air, as if something bad could happen. I got up and turned to the right and started walking out of the house. Then I could begin to hear some noise and I noticed that a bunch of young people were boogie boarding (like surfing). I grabbed a board and went in the water with them. I began to catch a beautiful wave, but as I looked down I noticed that the wave was going to end up on a grassy hill instead of the way waves normally end in the water. So I suddenly found myself, instead of continuing with the wave, flying in the air. It was a marvelous feeling and I continued for a while. Then I began to slowly come down to the ground. Then a voice inside me said to me, "You can do this. You can fly. Just feel what it is like to fly and continue." And I did."

If this is truly the day of peace and the unity of mankind, if the day of oneness has already come and is with us right now, then the days when we were isolated to our own home villages or towns for our whole life are over. When I first left my home at 18, I felt alone, as if I was in a big fog, isolated, wondering what bad thing was going to happen. Gradually I would get up and look to the future and start moving. Eventually, I would become enthusiastic and fly. It has always been the same experience for me. Each new city is like a different planet. Each new move is filled with loneliness and periods of isolation. It is only when I decide to get up and look to the future with an open mind that positive things happen, and I am excited to be in a new place.

For a long time, my tendency was to arrive in a new place and think about how great the last place was. There is a lot of comfort in the past, and when you are faced with uncertainty about the future, the past is suddenly glorious, and filled with great things. But over-glorifying the past is really a drug-like state for overcoming the fear of the future. There is only one way to go toward the future, with enthusiasm and encouragement. To be successful in the future one must be definite, without fear, and really looking forward. The future is only as fearful as our minds make it.

When I moved to Brazil, I didn't understand how strong the dynamic of loneliness would be. My first language is English; I spent nearly 50 years just speaking English. One day I flew from Los Angeles and the next day I landed in Brasilia. When you leave a place where you are comfortably communicating with others and then, the very next day, you are not able to have even the shortest of conversations, it feels like you are on another planet with strange creatures. A really funny thing happened to me the same day that I arrived in Brasilia. We went to our apartment and decided to take a nap. When I woke up, I decided to do what I often do in any new place. I decided to go out and take a run so that I could know the city better. I left the apartment looking around trying to notice some of the landmarks. I especially noticed a VW van in the parking lot. I had a plan to follow the road just off the main road, run on it for awhile, and then return. It was about 5:30 PM and, after about 20 minutes of running, it became dark. I was returning home, only now I was on the main road instead of the off road. As it was dark, I inadvertently ran past the place where I should have turned and found my self in a place that I didn't recognize at all. I stopped and walked a little to see if I could find the VW van. About an hour later, I was still walking looking for the van. There

I was, in a new country, unable to speak the language, in a city where every apartment building looks like every other apartment building, without an address or a telephone number, wondering how I was going to ever get home. I was really frightened. At the same time, although I didn't know this at the time, my wife had decided that she was not going to unpack anything because, fearing that I already might have been shot by a thief or something, she was going to get on the next plane back to America. After walking for an eternity, I noticed a place that had a few police cars, so I went in hoping they would give me help. I am certain that they thought I was from another planet, because I thought I was telling them that I was an American and lost, but I think I told them that I was an American and I was sorry. They were looking at me strangely; I had walked into a shelter for battered women. I asked them for a telephone book, but I couldn't read it, because I was wearing contact lenses for running that didn't allow me to focus at the near point for reading. Furthermore, they don't call the telephone listings "books," they call them lists. Finally, after taking out my contacts and finding a telephone number of someone at my work, I was rescued.

I truly had landed in a different world, and this was my baptism. The dream is trying to tell me the challenge and the solution. The challenge is my tendency is to sit in the fog and be lonely and self-conscious. The solution is rather easy. If I will just get up, move out of self-conscious isolation, and keep going forward, and I will do incredible things. Now if I could have done the end in the beginning, my initial moments in any new situation or place would be ecstatic. But as I was lost in the fog of fear and isolation, it took me some time to break free of the shackles of loneliness. The dream is telling me to just go ahead and fly. I don't need to hesitate.

There are countless ways to stay in the fog in a new place, and every one of them keeps a person from being truly helpful toward the process of peace. What I learn from this dream, is that doing incredible things requires leaving one's self-consciousness behind and turning toward enthusiasm. Every thought of worry or fear that makes one turn inside is a thought that impedes the process of more peace in the world. There are lots of reasons to stay in the house of one's ego and protect oneself and all of them are justifiable in one way or another, but none of them lead to peace. The only road to peace is the road of stepping out of one's self-consciousness and thinking and acting positively.

Positive thoughts are fundamental, because when you arrive in a new place, you are the novelty. You change the environment by your presence, because whatever was there before has a new element to it. If you have positive thoughts about positive change and higher states of unity, then your presence helps the environment to grow. If you think in a negative way by fearing or worrying, then you shut down the possibility that you can have a positive effect on the place and you actually become a detriment to growth. Unfortunately, many of us start in the state of self-consciousness, like I did in this dream. Wherever we go, we bring all of our fears and worries with us, as well as our hopes. The fears keep us in the fog, but step out of the fear into hope and enthusiasm, and you will soon be flying.

Why does this work? It works because of a basic principle: in the spiritual domain, all things are connected. You can say that one thing begets another and then you are flying, but it depends upon eliminating the fear of self-consciousness, moving forward, and relying on the guide inside yourself to show you the way. God can't help you if you are sitting still in the house of self-consciousness, but, as soon as you start moving forward, maintaining your enthusiasm and hope and awe, you will find yourself going from one amazing thing to another.

In principle, self-consciousness works like gravity. As long as you focus on the worry or the fear, you stay put and go more to the center of self. There is no escape; the worry keeps you in the center of your self. You can pray for a thousand years for someone to come along and pull you out of the miserable state, but it will be to no avail. Nothing can remove the worry or the fear until you step toward a positive, hopeful world. As soon as you focus on the positive world and take your mind off the worry, you are free, and then you fly. You can't fly and worry at the same time, because worrying negates positive energy. The solution is to find a way to move away from worry and into enthusiasm, this is how enthusiasm becomes a habit and worry disappears forever.

Every negative feeling, every weakness, exists in time and has a past. Every weakness is a temporary state, because it was created in time. There is an origin to negative states whether they be in the culture, in the familial patterns, or in the experience of life. On the other hand, every positive quality is permanent, because it exists outside of time and space. You can't unlearn a positive quality, you can only cover it up temporarily in the fog of self. Weaknesses will drop away, but qualities will remain.

So how do you get out of the fog and move into a state that leads to flying? If you know that negative things exist in time, one of the first things you can do is look for cues in time. For instance, you can ask the question, "When did this state of loneliness first begin for me?" Then you can answer the question by looking at some of the clues in the dreams. Time clues are often revealed by the ages of the people in the dream, and sometimes they are revealed by other clues. For instance, dinosaurs can mean something that happened long ago; ancient castles also suggest a long time ago. This dream addresses the birth of the positive stage. The stages of surfing and flying indicate that I learned those skills in adolescence, but it doesn't necessarily indicate the origin of the negative state. What gives the clue to the origin in this dream is that nothing is recognizable. It occurs in a strange planet, a strange house, and a foggy environment. This gives the clue that the origin is cultural. Culture is the hardest of all origins or patterns to change, because it is the most unconscious. You learn culture in almost the same way you learn to breathe. You don't know when it began, it just did. Every culture has its weaknesses as well as its strengths, and every society is working to overcome the weaknesses and turn them into strengths. The cultural pattern I revealed in the dream is that, when I am in a new place, I feel really isolated and alone.

Almost everyone in my home culture learns to feel this way in a new place, such as a new city, and a new country. The current dominant culture in my home country was founded predominantly by immigrants. When they came to the country, they couldn't speak the language, didn't have much money, and had left all of their friends and most of their family behind. When they came, they gathered together in their own language and cultural communities, so that they wouldn't feel so isolated. They worried that they wouldn't survive outside of their own community, so we learned to worry as soon as we left our communities. Many people feel extremely lonely when they leave their family or community or country. I did, too.

After moving away from home and living away for a year or so, I learned that all I had to do was step out of my room and start walking down the hall. I would end up doing something really interesting if I could just get excited and enthused about it. However, since I didn't know what I was doing, but had just stumbled upon it, the new pattern didn't last very long. Looking back, I can see that I felt the least lonely when I was the most enthusiastic. To get rid of the loneliness, I needed enthusiasm. When I go out the door and show enthusiasm, it is contagious, other people want to be with me. Then I have lots of friends, and I am doing things that I love to do.

For me, the formula for doing great things and for making more friends is to be enthusiastic about what lies ahead. Leave the lonely feelings at the door, because something great is out there waiting for all of us. We might even start flying.

Questions for meditation

1. Does keeping yourself away from others in new places make you feel strange? In what ways?
2. Analyze your close relationships. In what ways are they all similar?
3. Think about what you like to do. Make a list of the people that you have connected with as a result of doing those things.
4. Set a goal each day for doing something that you have never done before, and then do it.

Summary of symbols used

strange planet with fog—feeling strange in new places
body boarding—being on the cutting edge of human relationships;
        being able to do new things with others that are out of the
        ordinary for the culture flying—ease of doing the things you
        want to do
consciousness of how to fly—ease of knowing how to fly and then
        doing it

Commonality of symbols

The symbols progress from feeling lonely and unhappy to being together with others while you do the things you love to do; the joy of being with others and the joy of doing your favorite activities in life.

APPENDIX

METHODOLOGY OF ANALYZING AND
TRANSFORMING THE DREAMS

The methodology that I use to interpret and transform dreams comes from having a spiritual philosophy of life. This means that human beings are primarily spiritual in nature and that dreams arise out of non-material (spiritual) reality. Since humans are also material beings in that they have a physical body through which they pass this life, dreams are both representations of physical realities and spiritual realities.

The physical reality is locked in time and space which means that even though we are mainly spiritual, we live in the reality in time and in space. The dream world does not abide by the same rules of time and space because it exists outside of the physical world. This makes it possible for time and space to have different realities. For instance, the end can be in the beginning, the end and the beginning can be the same, or you can have neither beginning nor end. It also can mean that here is there, or here and there are the same, or that there is neither here nor there.

In a typically negative dream, time is often the reverse of what the reality of physical world is. The end (the purpose of the dream) comes at the beginning of the dream and the beginning (beginning of emotional and spiritual work) starts at the end. However a very positive dream has neither beginning nor end because it represents a spiritual energy that can be applied anywhere in one's life and produce excellent results.

Non-material (spiritual) positive reality has the power to automatically integrate with every other non-material positive energy. For instance, the energy of generosity automatically integrates with the energy of courage even though in their physical appearance they may seem very different and with unique objectives. The reason they are integrated is because all spiritual reality is one, that is, it is all connected and comes from the same source. It is only when it goes through the prism of human understanding that it takes on its differentiated reality. In other words the spiritual world is characterized by one unified force with infinite potentialities. When it appears in material form, it is in a differentiated form. We see, for instance, that a lion has the quality of courage and a tree the quality of uprightness. This differentiation in the material form allows us to have differentiated spiritual understanding so that we can use the information and the experiences we have for our own transformation.

Negative reality is, by nature, non-integrative. When you feel a negative emotion inside yourself, it means that you are not whole, not fully unified with yourself. When you feel a negative feeling such as fear or anxiety, recognize it origin, glean its understanding, and then transform it to its positive opposite, you become more unified with yourself. But just when you feel that the world is totally unified and you are at one with things, along comes another negative emotion to remind you that growth is endless and your journey has no end except higher and higher realizations of spiritual potentialities. Only the divine is perfect and wholly unified and we are subject to continual process of moving closer but never totally being unified.

When you understand that dreams are communication attempting to move you to higher levels of unity with your true self, you can free yourself from thinking negative dreams are bad and to be avoided or that it means that your are not a person full of positive energy. All dreams are just communication and when you understand them, they will help you grow and transform, become happier, more fulfilled, and accomplish your goals.

Why dreams are metaphorical?

The way we grow as human beings in the physical world has a lot to do with how we understand things. We become conscious that we do not have a certain ability, or are lacking an understanding in some area, by feeling incompetent or negative when we are facing certain challenges of life. Our minds and bodies tell us that something is not right and needs to develop. The thing we need to develop can appear as a positive image, but it is also stimulated in negative reality. Dreams are a way of telling us what is wrong or where we are going. The communication appears in metaphorical language so that we can understand the structure of the non-material reality we are facing and then change it. Since the spiritual world is infinite and unified, the dreams appear like a light going through a prism. When the spiritual world, which is unified, attempts to communicate with the human world, it sends the message through the prism of the mind in metaphorical language and when this language is understood, it can be transformed.

Structural Approach

When you are trying to understand a dream, it is very helpful to not let your everyday understanding of sequence and structure of the material reality interfere with what the dream is attempting to communicate. In the material world sequence follows the rules of the clock meaning time goes in a forward direction from beginning to middle to end. You wake up, you take a shower, you eat your breakfast, and then you go to work. In the dream world you could go to work and then wake up or you could eat your breakfast and then wake up or you could go to work and then take a shower. It all depends what the dream is trying to say. Waking up in a dream usually means moving from unconsciousness to consciousness. So often you hear a person say something like, "I had this terrible nightmare where a thief was chasing me trying to get my purse, and just when he was about to grab it, I woke up." This means that in your life you were asleep and you only woke up when the thief was about to grab you. We call this a wake up call, but it shows how in the dream world the waking up in one's life often comes after a really negative experience and the dream is a reflection of how this has happened and reflects the idea that dreams are telling you about internal reality in a perfect structure.

I often tell people that when I hear a dream, that I like to sit with it for awhile as if it is right next to me speaking to me. Then I do basically two things. Look at the metaphors and analyze the way the dream is presented. Both factors are critical. The metaphors are great, but they are not the end of the process. Where the metaphor is in the dream can be just as important as the metaphor itself.

Consider this example. "A huge bear was running after me and the faster I tried to go the slower I ran." It is easy enough to recognize that in the dream that a bear is a big strong negative energy coming after the person. But if you just understand the metaphors, you will still be fearful only you will also know what you are fearful of. When you understand the structure, you can transform it. The structure is that bear comes after me and then the faster I try to get away the worse it gets. The key words are after and faster. This means that to solve the dream, the slower you go beforehand, the more you will have the positive opposite of the bear, inner strength. Inner strength is gained by going inside and slowing way down so that you can take on the qualities of the bear. If you run away, things only get worse.

Here is another example. "I dreamt that I was walking down a dark alley and then a man started chasing me." In this dream the dreamer starts slow, but then gets faster. If you go slowly in dark narrow places in your life, places where there is no choice, something negative will happen. This is the structure. This means that positives happen when you give your self lots of choice and then your life lights up and you can run quickly.

Here is a positive dream sentence. "Walking through a dense forest." This could be a positive feeling for one person and a negative for another. The keys to the structure are walking through and density. Density means close together and walking means going slowly. So when she is slowed down with a lot of friends (close together) she is really positive. If you want this dreamer to be happy with you, take a slow walk in the forest with her or just slow way down and be with her. The key is getting close by slowing.

The structure is extremely important.

How to Interpret a Symbol

Example 1: A Shark

1. Ask yourself what a shark is and what are some of its characteristics.

    A shark is an animal that lives in the sea, has huge teeth, rips its prey by biting strongly into them, and has to have other smaller fish around to prey on.

2. Take one of the characteristics and ask yourself what that characteristic does.

    Teeth and jaw of a shark allow the shark to rip into the other.

3. Ask yourself what is the equivalent of a shark in the human non-material world.

    A shark is someone, positive or negative, who goes after something by attacking it with a huge grip and then ripping into it. Positive could be a way to go for new projects. Negative is a way to bring others down.

4. Ask yourself who the shark is in the dream.

    Is it your boss, your spouse, business associate, coach, your own self?

5. Keep asking more questions about the shark and the context of the dream.

What is the sea? The sea is the environment in which a shark lives. It is fluid which means that it has give and take like what is necessary in relationships, and it is huge which means it can have to do with the relationships with larger realities such as the divine.

6. Ask yourself how you need to be more like a shark in a positive way.

   Being like a shark would allow me to get a grip on my life, to rip through the negativity of myself and others, to attack the things that have always hampered me.

7. Imagine yourself as a positive shark.

8. Get assistance from appropriate professionals who can help you deal with how you have been a negative shark or how other sharks have ripped your life apart.

Example 2: A Mountain

A mountain is a high place from where you can see great distances. (vision) It can also be a thing you have to cross over or climb. (challenge) And it can also be a place of jumping from or skiing down. (courage)

What am I am not seeing? Where do I need more vision? What challenges am I facing? What keeps me from overcoming the obstacles? What fear is holding me from letting go and flying with things?

Imagine yourself on top of the mountain or overcoming obstacles or skiing down the mountain.

Example 3: A Snake

1. What is a snake?

   A snake is an animal that moves on the ground or in the water by conforming to the space it moves over. It takes the shape of whatever it moves over. It also sheds its old skin and some species have a poisonous venom.

2. What are the non-material equivalents of a snake in a positive or negative sense?

   Snakes have flexibility and because they are low to the ground and take the shape of things, reflect humility. They, therefore, are key symbols at the beginning of a transformation process because they reflect acceptance of whatever you have to go through to get to where you want to go. A poisonous snake can mean someone or something is poisoning your life such as listening to backbiting or gossip or a lot of negativity.

3. Who is the snake in your real life?

   If it is poisonous it usually reflects fear on your part caused by a jealous person. Jealousy is very venomous and causes people to act in destructive ways.

4. What is the context and details?

   For instance, if you feel positive, then it can mean you are in the beginning of a new change process and should go for it. If you are being constricted like with a boa constrictor or python, it can mean that you or someone else is preventing you from change by constricting your movement forward.

5. How can you be a snake in a positive way?

   Accept what you have to move through and go for it, instead of fighting it. The advantage of a snake which is the advantage of flexibility and humility is that you easily move through things by not trying to raise yourself above things or others, but by accepting others and accepting that you have lots to learn and move through.

6. Imagine yourself as a snake and how it helps you in your life now.

Example 4: Verbs—Running Away

Running away means that there is something that is chasing you which gives you fear. It is a verb instead of a noun.

What is the thing you are running away from?

This is always the key question. Who or what is giving you a lot of fear? It could an abusive person or an activity where you are going to get a lot of criticism.

What is the positive opposite of the thing you are running away from?

If you are running from a bear, the positive opposite is strength, from a lion, courage. It means that you need the positive opposite of the thing you are running away from and the thing you are running from is always the clue.

Imagine yourself as the positive quality such as a bear or a lion.

Seek assistance to get rid of the fear as you move more and more toward the positive quality. If you are running away from an abusive person, it means that you need a certain amount of empowerment, and it is going to be extremely valuable to find people such as a good therapist who can help you through the process.